RE-IMAGINING ACADEMIC LIBRARIES: A PERSPECTIVE ON INSTITUTIONAL REPOSITORIES

RE-IMAGINING ACADEMIC LIBRARIES: A PERSPECTIVE ON INSTITUTIONAL REPOSITORIES

Editors

Veeresh B. Hanchinal

Deputy Librarian
Tata Institute of Social Sciences
Tuljapur Campus, Tuljapur -413601
Dist. Osmanabad

Vidya V. Hanchinal

Librarian
J.M. Patel College of Commerce
Goregaon (W), Mumbai -400090

P Arul Pragasam

Librarian
Seva Sadan's College of Education
Opp. Central Hospital, Ulhasnagar -421003.
Dist. Thane

Ess Ess Publications

New Delhi

RE-IMAGINING ACADEMIC LIBRARIES : A PERSPECTIVE ON INSTITUTIONAL REPOSITORIES

ISBN: 978-81-7000-804-0

First Published 2016

Published by:
Ess Ess Publications
4831/24, Ansari Road,
Darya Ganj,
New Delhi-110 002.
INDIA
Phones: 23260807, 41563444
Fax: 41563334
E-mail: info@essessreference.com
www.essessreference.com

Cover Design by *Patch Creative Unit*

Printed and bound in India at Salasar Imaging Systems.

Contents

Preface

The open access movement has completely changed the scenario of publishing. It provides free access to information online without any restriction. The free availability of information on the Internet enables users to use lawfully is the revolution 21st century is witnessing. Because of this academic community is involved through their institutions in developing own institutional repositories to provide wide access to the scholarly resources. The Institutional Repository (IR) mainly consists of conference papers, theses and dissertations, technical reports, annual reports, working papers, govt. funded reports, peer-reviewed journal articles etc. These can be used freely for research, teaching, publication and not for profit purpose with proper acknowledgement.

IRs and Open Access Initiatives (OAI) are making significant developments in knowledge production and distribution. IR is an essential tool for scholarly communication in the digital age and IR's are increasingly deployed in academic institutions to manage a variety of digital content including educational, research and archival sources. There is a concentrated effort by the academic library community to build digital repository to preserve and give wide publicity to their institute's intellectual output online with free. In the era of ICT the IRs offers new possibilities for change and significant challenges as well to the libraries. The invited papers/

chapters are edited according to a stringent editorial review process and included in this book.

The first chapter "Open Access Publishing and Institutional Repositories: An Overview" by Lucy-A Tedd, introduces the concepts of open access publishing and institutional repositories. It provides an overview of projects being funded by the Joint Information Systems Committee within the UK in higher education institutions and information on how some of the outcomes of this work can be useful to those in other countries. It describes the progress of the Wales Repository Network in developing an integrated network of institutional repositories in Wales. Finally, it reports author's experiences in the use of an institutional repository at Aberystwyth University, Wales.

In Chapter 2, "Establishing Institutional Repositories: An overview" by Usha Mujoo Munshi, emphasizes the relevance of institutional repositories, benefits of institutional repositories at institutional & individual level, requirements and processes in setting up an institutional repository, economics of institutional repositories, planning, implementation and execution. It describes the significance of institutional repository to Indian academic & research organizations and discusses various strategies for the development of institutional repository with special reference to Indian institutions of higher learning.

Whereas, Chapter 3, "Developments of Institutional Repositories: An Overview" by Jayprakash, through light on challenges and opportunities in creating IRs, dwells on growth of IR at national and international level. It discusses national policy on IR, benefits and concludes that IR can serve as an engine of information transfer.

Chapter 4," New Metrics of Scholarly Communication and Emerging Roles of Academic Librarians: A case of Institutional Repositories" by Priti

Jain, explores how most academic *institutions* are *employing new* metrics of scholarship and communication to showcase and disseminate *research outputs today and how a*dvancement of new technologies has led to new emerging scholarly communication model known as open access (OA). It discusses the benefits and challenges of IRs; outlines IRs within the context of digital scholarship and highlights emerging roles of librarians in the successful execution of IRs. Finally, it puts forward some recommendations for the successful implementation of IRs.

In Chapter 5, "Institutional Digital Repositories: A platform to promote the Visibility & Impact of Institutional Research" by Sobhagyawati Gupta, describes essential elements of IR, contents of an Institutional Repository. It further, discusses key issues related to IR and importance of developing IR. The role of IR in improving visibility and Impact of Research is explained and lists various IR initiatives in India and describes the significant role of libraries in developing IR.

Chapter 6, "Institutional Repository: A Performance Indicator" by K. Chinnasamy, examines open source, open source system and need of developing institutional repository. It discusses necessary measures to be adopted while building IRs.

Chapter 7, "Building a Sustainable Institutional Repository: Some Guidelines" by N B Dahibhate and Sujata Hargude, describes Institutional Repository as an electronic archive of the scientific and scholarly outputs of an institution and the main aim behind development of Institutional Repository (IR). It is a type of content management system that holds the core intellectual assets of a university or college, and enables them to be used in a flexible way to support a variety of information business processes. The efforts are made to elaborate the process of development of IR for academic and research institutions using open access environment. And how an

IR plays an important role in archiving the intellectual collection and manuscripts of institution is well explained. It further, suggests various ways and means of sustainability.

Chapter 8, "Building an Institutional Repository: A Complete Installation Guide using SobekCM OSS" by Ali Akbar Petiwala, it describes in detail the process of building Institutional Repository using an Open Source Software, 'SobekCM' on Windows OS platform.

Chapter 9, "Potential and Prospects of Traditional Knowledge Digital Library (TKDL): A Call of Digital India" by Nidhi Dhawan, reports how the present day has changed from traditional to digital libraries, not only a technological progression but a transformation in the model by which people access and interact with information. It evokes the concern of conservation and protection of traditional knowledge of the developing countries in general and India in particular. It discusses various case studies and how TKDL has become a role model for developing countries.

Chapter 10, "Institutional Repositories- Awareness by Faculty of University of Thanjavur: A Case Study" by T. Narmadha, examines how flow of content is the preliminary requirement for development and sustenance and who are the main sources of the flow of content. However, it expresses the concern of low rate of participation of faculty members in IR. It reports the results of a survey among selected science and technology faculty members of Periyar Maniammai University of Thanjavur covering different aspects of IR. It also highlights the perceptions of faculty members regarding current copyright issues especially the issue of dual copyright.

Chapter 11, "Indian ETD Repositories in OpenDOAR: An Observation" by Jyotshna Sahoo, provides the state-of-the art of Institutional Repositories enlisted in OpenDOAR in the context of India. It explores the institutes listed and their share of contribution and what OSS is used by them. It further, investigates top ten organizations listed in OpenDOAR.

Chapter 12, "Initiatives of Digital Library Projects in India, UK and USA : An Overview" by Syeda Sarwat Farheen, dwells on how in the past libraries used to act as the storehouse of knowledge as resources available-mostly in printed form and how the library scenario is changing fast with the advent of digital technology and Internet connectivity. It further deals with the initiation of different library projects in India, UK and USA for digitization of libraries and the source of finance.

This volume is designed to serve the core purpose of those who would like to venture out in building institutional repository for their institution/organization and also to the community who would like to study and understand the benefits of self publishing of scholarly work.

We are highly indebted to Prof. C R Karisiddappa for his words of wisdom in the form of "Foreword" to this volume. He has always been the great source of inspiration to us.

The editors offer sincere thanks to Prof Lucy Tedd and Inflibnet for their permission to include the article in this volume. Editors also thank Dr. Usha Munshi for her permission to include her scholarly paper. We place on record our special thanks to all the authors for contributing their scholarly research papers/chapters. Sincere thanks are extended to Ess Ess Publications, New Delhi for elegant printing and publication of the book.

— Editors

Foreword

"Access to Information is a Human Right, but it is often treated as a Privilege. This has to Change – and it will take all of us to make it Happen." ***— Erin McKiernan***
Open Access Advocate

The world is witnessing a rapid increase in the output of scholarly information which is embodied in various formats. The developments in electronic communication through internet, now offers libraries and researchers an opportunity to change fundamentally the way scholarly content is communicated. In the earlier years, journals were considered as the only sources of scholarly communication. In the course of time, commercial publishersstarted gaining maximum mileage by raising the cost of subscriptions beyond the reach of the libraries. The escalation of subscription cost of journals forced the libraries even the major ones, to cancel the subscriptions due to affordability issue and thus depriving access of scholarly content to their users. Budapest Open Access Initiative, a pioneering effort in popularizing the open access movement rightly declared that "free availability on public internet permitting any user to read, download, copy, distribute, print, search or link to the full texts of these articles, crawl them for indexing, pass these as data to software or use them for any other lawful purpose without financial, legal or technical barriers other than those inseparable from gaining access to the internet itself." In fact, this declaration inspired a number of institutions and organizations to develop the Institutional Repositories. Institutional Repository by definition means 'a digital archive of the intellectual assets created by the faculty, research staff and students of an institution and accessible to end users both within and outside the institution'.

Reitz Joan has rightly said 'An Institutional Repository (IR) serves as an indicator of the scope and extent of the university's research activities.' India is on the threshold of information bloom in academic institutions. Institutional Repositories (IRs) in India are gaining momentum. Over 60 institutional repositories have been setup in India during the last decade. Impetus for this growth is easy availability of good number of open source software for setting up repositories and the overwhelming support from the professional organisations. It is heartening to note that UGC has been encouraging universities to set up IRs by providing funding support under major projects.

The present publication entitled "*Re-imagining Academic Libraries: A perspective on Institutional Repositories,*" is an edited volume of 12 papers contributed by experienced library and information science teachers and practitioners. Each paper is an outcome of a systematic study and research. There are some case studies, perspective presentations, overviews and also installation guidelines. A publication of this type is very helpful to know the state-of-the-art of IRs, especially in the Indian context. At the same time, these contributions are guiding the future generation of library and information professionals in setting up the IRs and advance the open access movement. In fact, this volume will be a good addition to the LIS literature. I am happy that the editors have planned this timely publication. I wish editors a great success and hope it inspires more studies and research in the field of IRs. My sincere thanks to the editors for the kind gesture of giving me an opportunity to pen the foreword to this book.

To summarize, the IRs have brought a change in scholarly communication at institutional level and help bringout the hidden treasures in the form of research output lying low in various print and other storage formats. I wish this would usher in the long term preservation of scholarly contribution of an institution with wider access which in turn, would showcase the intellectual output of the institution. I would reiterate Alexander Graham Bell's words that 'The achievement of one goal should be the starting point of another' and wish that the editorial team brings out many more valuable publications in the future.

Prof. C. R. Karisiddappa
Former Professor and Chairman
Visiting Professor(2011-2015)
Emeritus Professor(2008-2010)
Department of Library and Information Science
Karnatak University,
Dharwad-580 003

About the Contributors

Ali Akbar Petiwala, is a Librarian at RBK School, Mumbai. He has also worked as Librarian with two more reputed schools of Mumbai; Campion School and Euro School and with Institute of Business School, Mumbai a prestigious institute in management studies in Mumbai region. He has also worked as Technical Assistant, INFLIBNET Centre for widely used SOUL 2.0 Library Software in Maharashtra & Goa region. He has published Three papers in national & international journals. His subjects of interest are Open Source Software, Institutional Repository, Digital library etc.

Jayaprakash, Ph.D., is presently working as a Librarian at Dnyanprassarak Mandal's College and Research Center, Assagao, Mapusa, Goa. He served two decades as a Librarian in different professional college; Nursing, Medical, Dental, Engineering, Pharmacy colleges. He has participated, presented and published 35 papers in National and International conferences and journals. Dr. Jayaprakash is also a member of professional associations like ILA, IASLIC, KALA, and IATLIS.

Jyotshna Sahoo, Ph.D., is currently serving as a Lecturer in the P.G. Department of Library and Information Science, Sambalpur University,Odisha. She holds a Bachelor degree in Education, M.A. in History, MLISC. and Ph.D. in Library & Information Science from

Utkal University, Odisha. Prior to her joining in teaching, she has had served as the Asst. Librarian of Odisha's Premier Institutional Culture Heritage, 'Odisha State Museum' for More than a decade. Preservation and conservation documentary heritage, Knowledge Organisation, Library management, Academic research relevance fall under the ambit of her area of interest. She has authored two books and 30 research papers published in different journals of national and international repute. She was awarded (i) UGC-NET in Library and Information Science-1998; (ii) Junior Research Fellowship from Department of Culture, Govt. of India-2007; (iii) ICSSR Doctoral Fellowship for the Ph.D. work-2007; (iv) Project Director of ICSSR project entitled "Mapping of Research Productivity in the fields Social Sciences in Odisha". She is the Life Member professional bodies like, ILA, IASLIC.

K. Chinnasamy, Ph.D. Head, Dept of Library and Information Science, Madurai Kamaraj University, Madurai-Tamil Nadu, India is a renowned library and information science teacher has had a good academic record for more than three decades. In his diverse professional career in the library as well as teaching library and information science and guided more than 25 Ph.ds and 83 M.Phil scholars from various reputed universities. Throughout his academic career he had participated actively in international, national and regional conferences organized by different agencies of higher education and published more than 52 papers and visited many countries. He was an instrumental for Library and information Science programmes in distance education in Alagappa University, Karaikkudi, Tamilnadu. He has vast expertise as resource person for seminars at various levels and acted as external referee for viva voce of research for many universities of southern state. He is an active member of the administrative boards of several professional educational institutions and served as

Additional Controller of Examination in Madurai kamaraj University and subject expert for various selection committee bodies of the universities and higher educational institutions. He has honoured by many institutions for his professional achievement.

Lucy Tedd is an Emeritus Lecturer in the Department of Information Studies at Aberystwyth University, Wales. In 2014 she was honoured to receive the Jason Farradane Award for her "sterling work as an international advocate for the information profession throughout her career, both within education and in the wider library and information profession". Lucy was involved in teaching and research at Aberystwyth from 1972 until her retirement in 2012, and has been a prolific author of research and professional reports, articles, and books, including internationally established standard textbooks such as *An introduction to computer-based library systems, Digital Libraries Principles and Practice in a Global Environment* (with Andrew Large), and *Information seeking in the online age: principles and practice* (with Andrew Large and Richard Hartley). Lucy was the Editor of Emerald's international journal *Program: electronic library and information systems* from 1984-2011 and was presented with an Outstanding Service Award by the Emerald Literati Network to acknowledge her exceptional work. Lucy was a frequent participant at international conferences both in the UK, Europe , India, South East Asia, Australia and South America.

Nandkumar B. Dahibhate, Ph.D. Ex. Principal Technical Officer, CSIR- National Chemical Laboratory, Pune, has more than Four decades of working experience in special library system. He has delivered number of guest lecturers for B Lib, M Lib, M Phil, PGDLAN courses & PhD programmes in various universities. He is a visiting faculty in Tilak Maharashtra Vidyapeeth, Pune and adjunct professor in Shivaji University, Kolhapur. He has guided number of M.Phil & Ph. D. students. He is member of BOS, RR committee, selection committee of various universities. He has received many awards; "Granth Mitra Purraskar" by Parnerkar Maharaj Granthalaya and Public library, Parner, Maharashtra, "Certificate of Excellence" in recognition of exemplary contributions in Library and Information Science, by Karnataka State SC/ST Professional Association (R) Gulbarga, Karnataka, "Sammaan Patra" from Council of Scientific and Industrial Research (CSIR) New Delhi, for appreciation towards contribution of services to CSIR etc. He has actively involved in developing specialized scientific databases. He has published One book and more than 60 scholarly papers in various national/international conference proceedings & journals.

Nidhi Gauba Dhawan, Ph.D., is presently working as an Assistant Professor at Amity Institute of Environmental Sciences (AIES) at Amity University Uttar Pradesh, Noida. She has significantly contributed to the field of Environmental Sciences through her Research and Teaching. She has worked on development of agrotechniques for medicinal plants under variable environmental stresses. She has written research papers in various journals of National and International repute and has also presented papers in various International conferences. She has three books to her credit. She teaches environmental studies to the undergraduates & post graduate students. She specializes in the area of Ecology and Environmental Botany, Plant Ecology, Biodiversity, Natural Resources Management, Intellectual Property Rights (IPR) and Ethnobotany.

Priti Jain, currently she is an Associate Professor in the Department of Library and Information Studies at the University of Botswana. She holds B.A (Hons) and LL.B degrees from Meerut University, India, Masters in Library and Information Studies from the University of Botswana, and D Lit. et Phil (Doctor of Literature and Philosophy) from the University of South Africa (UNISA).

During her15 years working experience in Library and Information Science discipline, Priti has published widely in renowned refereed journals and book chapters, and has presented over 30 papers in international conference. She teaches and supervises students at undergraduate, Masters and Ph.D levels in areas of Knowledge Management and Library Information Science. Her current areas of interest are: Knowledge management, Open access, Institutional Repository, and Digital Scholarship.

Sobhagyawati Gupta is working as In-Charge Library and Assistant Librarian at Central University of Rajasthan, Kishangarh, Ajmer (Rajasthan). Before joining the Central University of Rajasthan, she has worked about 4 years in Banasthali University. She has done MLISc from University of Rajasthan, Jaipur in 2003 and M.A. (Pub. Admn.) in 2005. She is gold medalist in MLISc. She has also qualified UGC NET-JRF in June, 2008. She has presented many papers in various national and international conferences and published 15 articles in journals and books. She is also co-editor of a National Journal in Hindi 'Granthalya Vigyan' since 2014.

Sujata S. Hargude is working in Tilak Maharashtra Vidyapeeth, Pune since 2006. She has Five years experience of teaching BLIS & MLIS programmes. She has acquired M.Phil degree in the year 2015. She has presented and published Four research papers in various conferences/seminars and also attended workshops. Her area of specialization is; Information science, ICT, Digital Libraries.

Syeda Sarwat Farheen is working as Librarian at J.S.P.M.'s Mahila Kala Mahavidyalaya Aurangabad (Maharashtra). She has done M. L. I. Sc. from Dr. Babasaheb Ambedkar Marathwada University, Aurangabad in 2007. She has qualified UGC NET in June 2007 and SET in January 2008. She has presented many papers in various state, national and international conferences and written many articles in national and international journals.

T. Narmadha, Ph.D., is working as a Periyar Maniammai University in the Department of Library and Information Science, Thanjavur. She has obtained M.A., MLIS and M. Phil (LIS) from Annamalai University, and Alagapa Unvinversity, & Ph.D. from Bharathidasan University. Prior to this, she was Director Library at Periyam Maniammai, Thanjavur. She has published many papers in different journals and conference proceedings.

Usha Mujoo Munshi, Ph.D., a Fulbright Scholar is currently with Indian Institute of Public Administration (IIPA). She has over 155 research publications and few books to her credit. She is a recipient of several national and international awards; Raizada Memorial Award 1994 for Young Information Scientist of the Society of Information Science (SIS); SIS Fellowship in 1999; Fulbright Scholar in 1996-97. ASSIST International Best Paper Award by ASSIST, USA in 2002. In 2009, Dr. Munshi obtained post of DEA (directeur d' etudes associe), she is the first person to receive this recognition in the area of Information Science and Technology by Foundation Maison des sciences de l'homme, Paris, (France). She is on the editorial board of various national/ international journals and she has been nominated as a member for the Steering Committee of IAP (Inter Academy Panel) and Task force on Digital Resources - US National Academy of Sciences, USA and Co-Chair, Steering Committee, National Digital Preservation Programme (NDPP). She has been nominated as member international "Data Policy Committee" (a four member international committee) by CODATA (International Council for Science (ICSU)), Paris. She has been associated with the Consultative Development Committee – set up by the Department of Science and Technology (DST), Govt. of India for the Preparation of "Strategic Road Map for Data Analytics" for the Government. She has also been on the panel of International Scientific Programme Committee of the SciDataCon2014 of CODATA, Paris and the World Data System, Japan. Her area of interest include- information extraction, IR, knowledge management, digital libraries and research mapping.

List of Tables

List of Figures

List of Annexures

1

Open Access Publishing and Institutional Repositories : An Overview

Lucy A Tedd

DEFINITION OF TERMS

Open Access

In recent years many librarians and academic authors have become concerned at what is seen as the 'commercialisation' of scholarly journal publishing and the requirement for authors to sign over the copyright of a paper to the publishers prior to publication. Libraries need to pay increasingly large sums to subscribe to the printed copies of the journals or to acquire licences for access to electronic versions of them or else cancel subscriptions which results in researchers failing to have access to necessary source materials. The result has been a growth of the 'open access' movement.

In the UK the Joint Information Systems Committee (JISC) produced a briefing paper on open access in 2006 where it stated that:

"The World Wide Web has provided the means for

researchers to make their research results available to anyone, anywhere, at any time. This applies to journal articles regardless of whether or not their library has a subscription to the journal in which the articles were published as well as to other types of research output such as conference papers, theses or research reports. This is known as Open Access." (http://www.jisc.ac.uk/publications/publications/ pub_openaccess_v2.aspx).

A major 'mover and shaker' in the OA world is Stevan Harnad of Southampton University in the UK. He states that OA is the "free, immediate, permanent online access to the full text of research articles for anyone, webwide" (http:// www.eprints.org/openaccess/). In 1995 Harnad made what became known as his 'subversive proposal' leading to the open access vision for scholarly material (Harnad, 1995). Since then there have been various international initiatives to progress the case for open access publishing. One of these was the Budapest Open Access Initiative (BOAI) of 2001 which resulted from a meeting organised by the Open Society Institute. Since 1993 the OSI in Budapest has developed and implemented a number of programmes in the areas of educational, legal and social reform in former Soviet republics and countries of central and eastern Europe. OSI's Information Programme has supported a number of projects relating to open access including:

- the development of business models and plans for self-archiving and open access publishing;
- the use of library networks to mobilise support for open access;
- support for authors in low and middle income countries to publish in open access journals;
- the development of software tools and templates for open access publishing, self-archiving , indexing and navigation;
- the promotion of the open access philosophy.

The BOAI states that:

"An old tradition and a new technology have converged to make possible an unprecedented public good. The old tradition is the willingness of scientists and scholars to publish the fruits of their research in scholarly journals without payment, for the sake of inquiry and knowledge. The new technology is the internet. The public good they make possible is the world-wide electronic distribution of the peer-reviewed journal literature and completely free and unrestricted access to it by all scientists, scholars, teachers, students, and other curious minds. Removing access barriers to this literature will accelerate research, enrich education, share the learning of the rich with the poor and the poor with the rich, make this literature as useful as it can be, and lay the foundation for uniting humanity in a common intellectual conversationand quest for knowledge."

In 2003 a conference on open access to knowledge in the sciences and the humanities was held in Berlin with an outcome that has become known as the Berlin Declaration (http://oa.mpg.de/ openaccess-berlin/ berlindeclaration.html) and follow-on conferences have been held annually. The declaration states that: "the Internet offers the chance to constitute a global and interactive representation of human knowledge , including cultural heritage and the guarantee of worldwide access and that this challenge needs to be addressed through content and software tools that must be openly accessible and compatible".

There are two roads to OA publishing:

a) Gold OA. In this situation OA journals use a funding model that does not charge readers or their institutions for access. The Directory of Open Access

Journals (DOAJ) is maintained by Lund University in Sweden and in early 2009 included details of 3,854 full-text, quality controlled scientific and scholarly journals, with 90 being categorised as being in the Library and Information Science area (examples include Ariadne, D-Lib Magazine and First Monday).

b) Green OA. In this case, authors publish papers in one of the 25,000 or so refereed journals in all disciplines and then self-archive these papers in open access repositories. Green OA publishing is aimed at making peer-reviewed research accessible to all through digital repositories which might be subject-based, or based within institutions.

Oppenheim has written a good overview paper outlining the situation, in 2008, with scholarly publishing and open access. In his conclusion he notes that "Libraries will increasingly switch to OA sources, leading to libraries gaining a more prominent role in scholarly publishing with activity in both the preservation and distribution of scholarly research. Libraries will need to move from being passive to active players in the scholarly communication chain". Work in this area is also carried out by the Scholarly Publishing and Academic Resources Coalition (SPARC), and SPARC Europe. SPARC was developed by the Association of Research Libraries in the US with a focus is to stimulate the emergence of new scholarly communication models that expand the dissemination of scholarly research (*http://www.arl.org/sparc/*).

Institutional Repositories

Writing in 2003, Clifford Lynch, the Executive Director, Coalition for Networked Information in the US, noted that; "In my view, a university-based institutional repository is a set of services that a university offers to the members of its community for the management and dissemination of digital materials created by the institution and its community members. It is most essentially an organizational commitment to the stewardship of these digital materials, including long-term preservation where appropriate, as well as organization and access or distribution." There are other definitions as given in Charles Bailey's Introduction to institutional repositories. In its entry for institutional repositories Wikipedia states that: "An Institutional Repository is an online locus for collecting, preserving, and disseminating, in digital form, the intellectual output of an institution, particularly a research institution. The four main objectives for having an institutional repository are:

- to create global visibility for an institution's scholarly research;
- to collect content in a single location;
- to provide open access to institutional research output by self-archiving it;
- to store and preserve other institutional digital assets, including unpublished or otherwise easily lost ("grey") literature (e.g., theses or technical reports). http://en.wikipedia.org/wiki/Institutional_repositories

An institutional repository differs from other digital collections that might be offered by a university library (such as access to ebooks, e-journal etc.) as:

- Content is deposited in a repository by the creator, owner and so on.
- Repository architecture manages the content and the metadata
- Repository software offers a minimum set of basic services – put, get, search
- Repository must be sustainable, trusted, well supported and well-managed (Heery and Anderson, 2005).

Subject-based repositories of e-prints were pioneered in 1991 by Paul Ginsparg at the Los Alamos National Research Laboratory in New Mexico with a collection of preprints of articles in the subject area of high energy physics. This collection, known as arXiv, is now based at Cornell University (http://arxiv.org) and has grown to include over 520,000 e-prints in Physics, Mathematics, Computer Science, Quantitative Biology, Quantitative Finance and Statistics.

In the 2000s work began in various academic institutions in creating their own repositories of e-prints. An institutional repository is a tangible indicator of research output of a university – thus increasing its visibility, prestige and public value. An IR can also be used as a marketing tool for the institution and allows an institution to manage its Intellectual Property Rights appropriately. Southampton University in the UK was an early developer and it produced software known as eprints (Simpson, 2006). In the US the Massachusetts Institute of Technology (MIT) with Hewlett Packard developed other software, DSpace. Both of these are still popular choices for any institution currently developing an IR.

The range of material that might be covered by an IR includes:

- Pre-prints of papers
- Post-prints of papers
- Doctoral theses
- Masters dissertations
- Research reports
- Book chapters
- Conference papers
- Teaching materials
- Databanks of 'raw' data
- Multimedia objects

In a 2009 report on the research library's role in digital repository services written by a task force for the Association of Research Libraries in North America it was suggested that research libraries should undertake the following actions with respect to digital repositories:

- Build a range of new kinds of partnerships and alliances, both within institutions and between institutions.
- Base service-development strategies on substantive assessment of local needs rather than blindly replicating work done at another institution.
- Engage with key local policy issues and stakeholders to encourage institutional engagement with national and international policy issues.
- Develop outreach and marketing strategies that assist "early adopters" of repositories to connect with the developing repository-related service system.
- Define a scope of responsibility to guide the development of repository services for varied forms of content.

EXAMPLES OF INSTITUTIONAL REPOSITORIES

CADAIR at Aberystwyth University (*http://cadair.aber.ac.uk/*)

Work on the development of an IR at Aberystwyth started in 2006. DSpace was chosen as an open source solution with a member of staff within Information Services (a central facility covering library services and computing facilities) responsible for its development. A repository manager was appointed in 2008 whose role is to assist in populating the repository. In early 2009 there were 1763 items included, mainly journal articles and conference presentations with some theses and dissertations. Figure 1.1 shows part of the opening page of CADAIR with the number of items included from various departments.

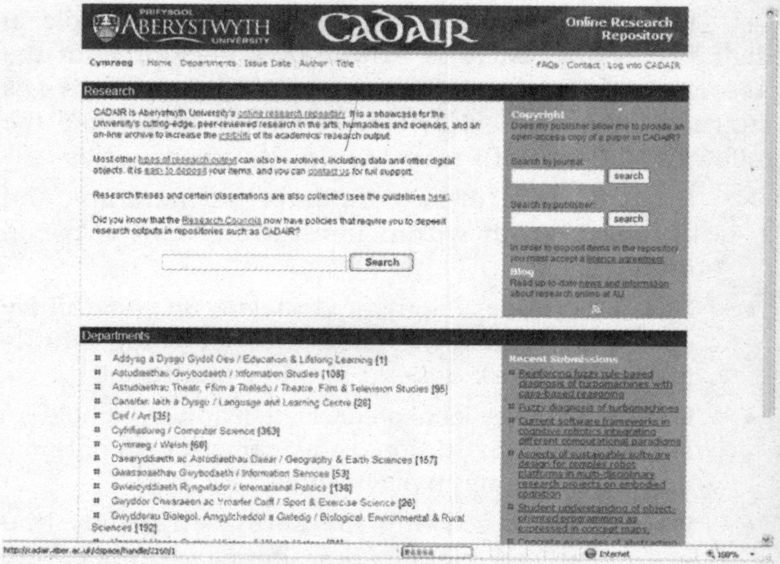

Fig. 1.1. Opening page of CADAIR

Figure 1.2 shows the metadata of a CADAIR item covering a conference presentation I made at the National Institute for Fashion Technology in India last year.

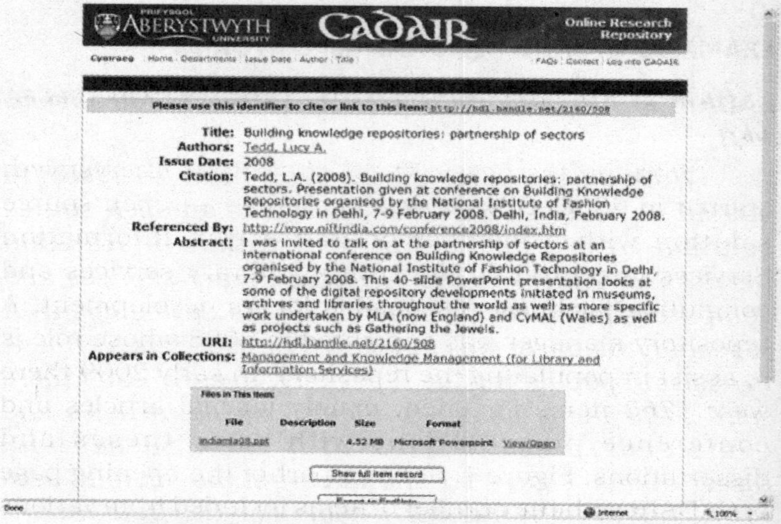

Fig. 1.2. Metadata for an item in CADAIR

A click on the file name will give access to the full presentation – which is no longer available on the Nift India website. Figure 1.3 gives the start of the full text of a paper published in Program: Electronic Library and Information Systems.

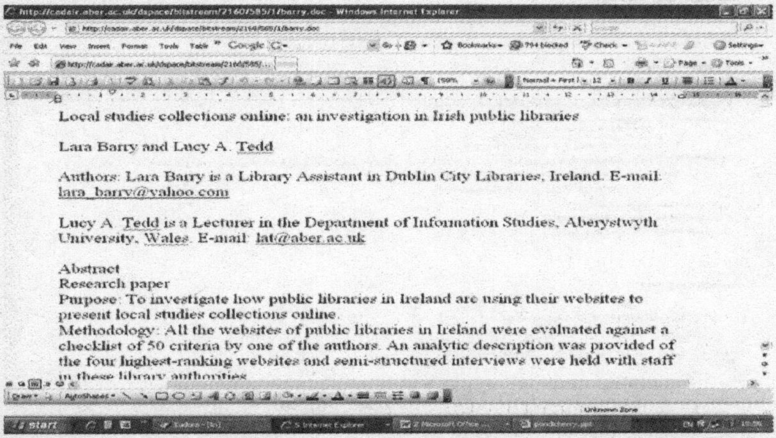

Fig. 1.3. Start of the full text of a paper in a refereed journal

It can be seen that the paper shown in Figure 1.3 is not as it would look in its final version in the Emerald-published journal and is a post-print i.e. it is the version of the paper as submitted for publication after the necessary referencing process and editorial changes. Publishers vary in their policies regarding the ability for an author to selfarchive material. Emerald is (appropriately) categorised as a 'green' publisher by the SHERPA RoMEO service and the rules regarding selfarchiving are shown in the record for Emerald in Figure 1.4. The development of the colour-coding system for publishers with respect to their policies for self-archiving by authors is described by Jenkins et al. (2007).

DSpace is a popular choice for IRs in India too. Mittal and Mahesh (2008) provide details of some 22 organisations using DSpace in 2007. One of those was the National Institute of Ocenaography (NIO), which at the time of Mittal and Mahesh's survey had 627 items in its collection and by early 2009 this had grown to 2552. Figure 1.5 shows the opening page of the NIO digital repository.

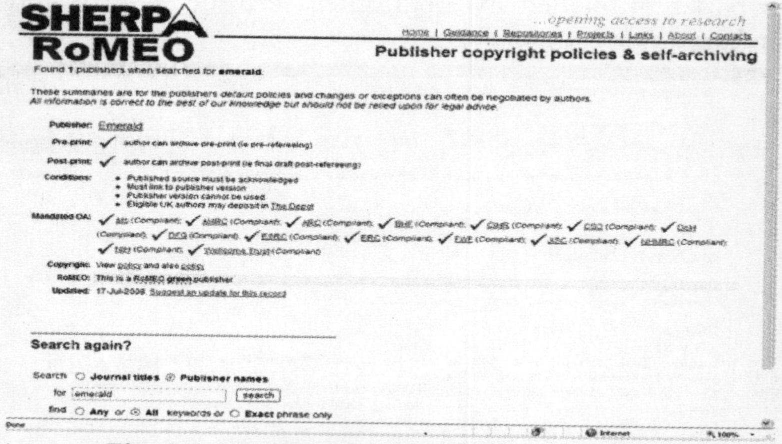

Fig. 1.4. Information regarding the publisher Emerald on the SHERPA RoMEO service

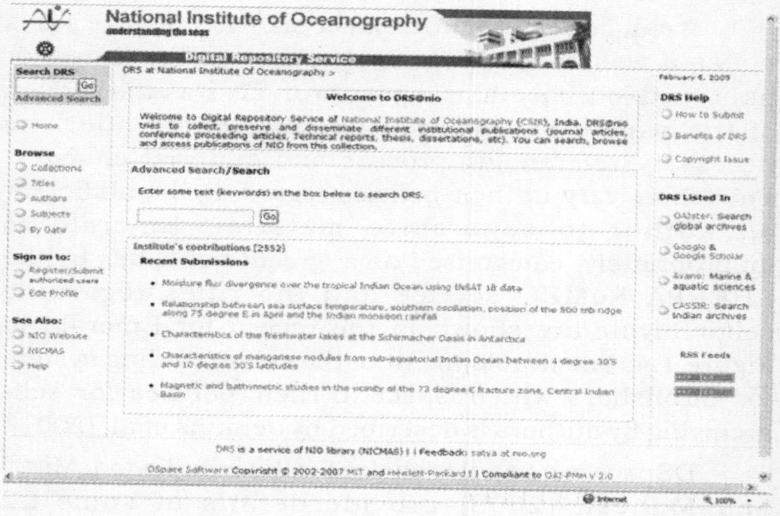

Fig. 1.5. Opening page of National Institute of Oceanography Digital Repository Service

Figure 1.6 shows the results of browsing for the most recent entries in the Biological Sciences collection and it can be seen that there is a mixture of doctoral theses and articles published in journals.

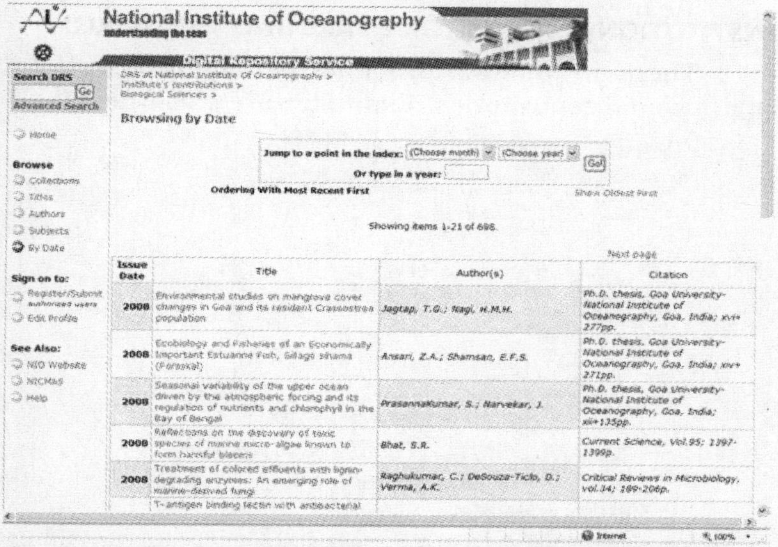

Fig. 1.6. Results of browsing recent entries in the Biological Sciences collection of the NIO repository

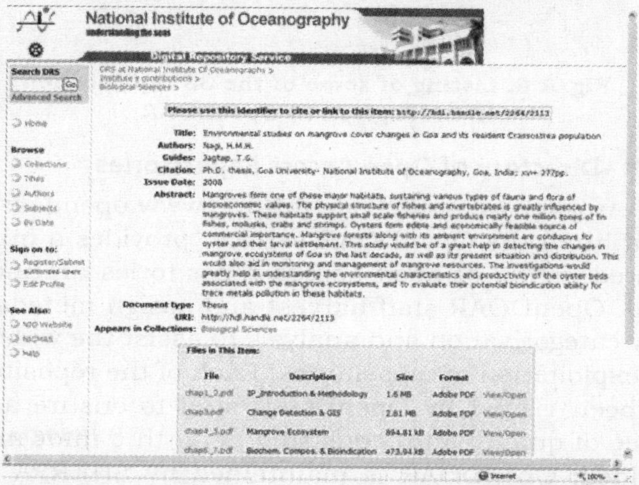

Fig. 1.7. Example of the metadata for a PhD thesis

The metadata for the first thesis is given in Figure 1.7 and it can be seen how easy it would be for anyone around the world to now gain access to the full text of this research.

INSTITUTIONAL REPOSITORIES AROUND THE WORLD

There are now various international directories of institutional repositories. Examples are given here.

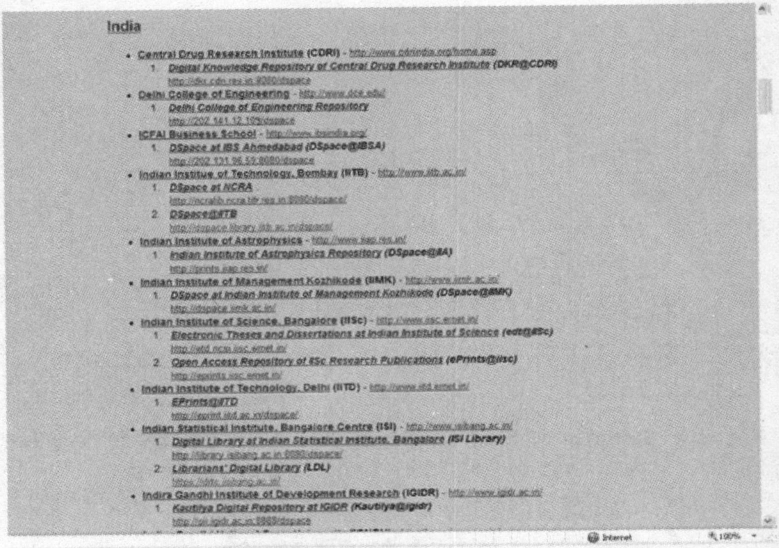

Fig. 1.8. Listing of some of the 33 repositories in India given in OpenDOAR

DOAR –Directory of Open Access Repositories

As given on its website (http://www.opendoar.org/about.html) the OpenDOAR service "provides a quality-assured listing of open access repositories around the world. OpenDOAR staff harvest and assign metadata to allow categorisation and analysis to assist the wider use and exploitation of repositories. Each of the repositor ies has been visited by OpenDOAR staff to ensure a high degree of quality an d consisten cy in th e infor mation provided: OpenDOAR is maintained by SHERPA". The work of the OpenDOAR team at Nottingham University in the UK is funded by a number of organisations including the OSI, the JISC, the Consortium of Research Libraries (CURL) and SPARC Europe. There are currently 1300 repositories covered by OpenDOAR. Some of the 33 in India are shown in Figure 1.8.

A chart showing the breakdown by country is given in Figure 1.9.

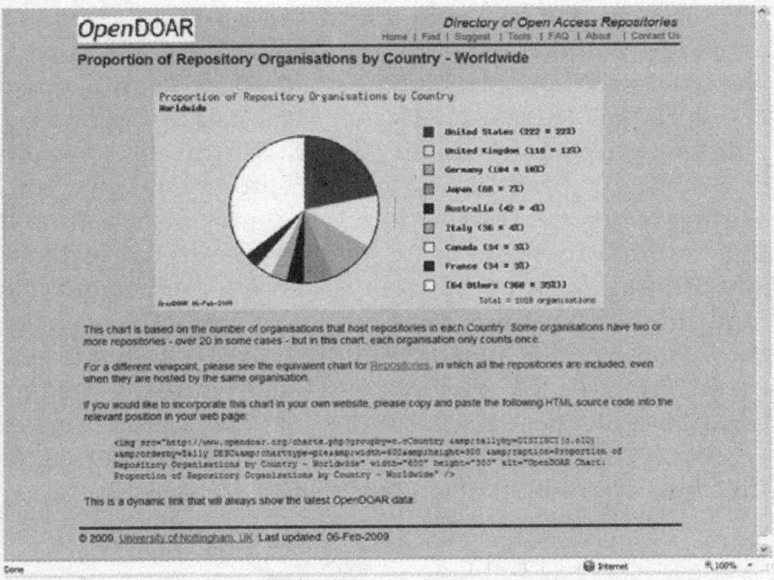

Fig. 1.9. Pie chart showing brea kdown of repository organisations in different countries.

ROAR – Registry of Open Access Repositories

ROAR is a parallel project to OpenDOAR and runs at Southampton University in the UK. It currently has 1247 entries, 40 of which are from India. Figure 10 shows some of the details included in ROAR for some Indian IRs. According to its website (http://trac.eprints.org/projects/iar/wiki) ROAR aims to "promote open access to the research literature pre- and post-peer-review through author self-archiving in institutional eprint archives. Open access to research maximises research access and thereby also research impact, making research more productive and effective.

This registry has two functions: (1) to monitor overall growth in the number of eprint archives and (2) to maintain a list of GNUEPrints sites (the software Southampton University has designed to facilitate self-archiving".

ROAR also keeps track of the archiving policies adopted by universities, funding bodies and so on with respect to authors depositing material in open a ccess repositories (http://www.eprints.org/openaccess/policysignup/). By February 2009, 31 universities and departments (including Southampton, Glasgow and Stirling in the UK, Harvard and Stanford in the US, and the National Institute of Technology, Rourkela in India and Bharathidasan University) had adopted mandates requiring that authors they fund and employ to deposit the output of their research in open access repositories. In addition there were 34 research funding bodies (including all the UK Research Councils, the European Research Council and the US National Institutes of Health) that now operate similar mandates.

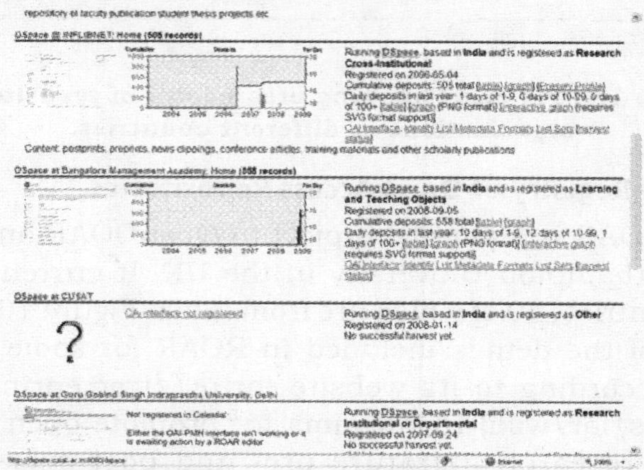

Fig. 1.10. Shows some of the details included in ROAR

Ranking of World Repositories

The Ranking of World Repositories is produced by the Cybermetrics Lab, a research group belonging to the Consejo Superiorde Investigaciones Científicas (CSIC), the largest public research body in Spain. One of the specific areas of research undertaken by CSIC is quantitative studies about the scientific communication through electronic journals and repositories, and the impact of the OA initiatives. The aim of the ranking is, as stated on the website (http://repositories.webometrics. info/about _ rank.html) to "support Open Access initiatives and therefore the free access to scientific publications in an electronic form and to other academic material. The web indicators are used here to measure the global visibility and impact of the scientific repositories". Figure 1.11 includes some of the listing of the 556 repositories (including CADAIR) covered in this directory.

Fig. 1.11. Alphabetic listing from the Ranking of World Repositories

Various web indicators are then used to rank the repositories:

- Size (S). Number of pages recovered from Google, Yahoo, Live Search and Exalead.
- Visibility (V). The total number of unique external links received (inlinks) by a site can be on ly con fidently obtained fr om Yahoo Search and Exalead.
- Rich Files (R). Only the number of text files in Acrobat format (.pdf) extracted from Google and Yahoo are considered.
- Scholar (Sc). Using Google Scholar database to calculate the mean of the normalised total number of papers and those (recent papers) published between 2001 and 2008.

The four ranks are then combined according to a special formula which results in the ranking as seen in Figure 1.12.

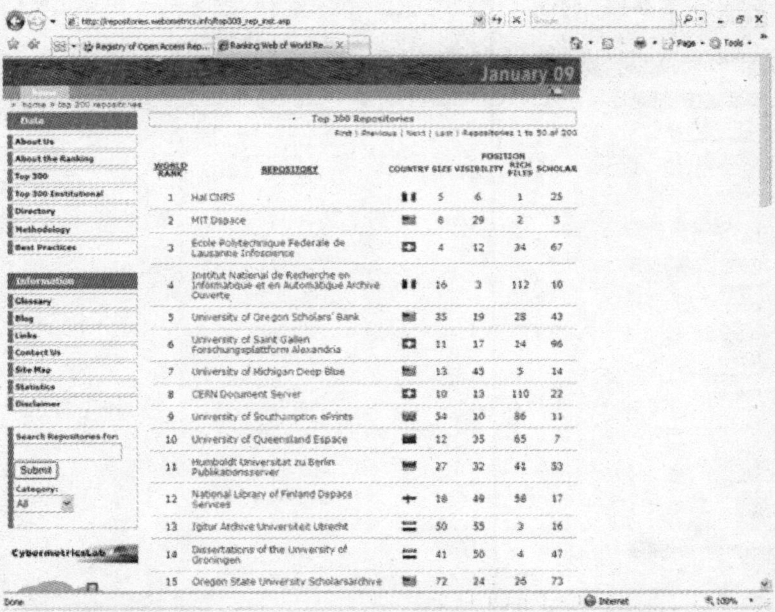

Fig. 1.12. World ranking of institutional repositories

JISC AND INSTITUTIONAL REPOSITORIES

The JISC (http://www.jisc.ac.uk) is funded by the UK higher education (HE) and further education (FE) bodies to provide world-class leadership in the innovative use of ICT to support education and research. In particular its work covers:

- The Joint Academic Network (JANET) which links all HE and FE establishments to the Internet
- Access to electronic resources
- New environments for learning, teaching and research
- Guidance on institutional change
- Advisory and consultancy services (e.g. Technical Advisory Service for Images, TechDIS for information on technology and disability).

JISC has had a number of funding programmes, as described below, linked to the development of institutional repositories and continues in this work through a current call for proposals for funding. The JISC - Repositories mailing list (JISC-REPOSITORIES@JISCMAIL.AC.UK) provides a lively discussion forum for those interested in the work of JISC and repositories.

Focus on Access to Institutional Repositories (FAIR) 2002-5

This programme (http://www.jisc.ac.uk/whatwedo/programmes/fair.aspx) started with a call for proposals in February 2002 which asked for projects to "support access to and sharing of institutional content within HE and FE and to allow intelligence to be gathered about the technical, organizational and cultural challenges of these processes". This resulted in 14 projects including:

- Rights Metadata for Open Archiving (RoMEO)
- Secured Hybrid Environment for Research, Preservation and Access (SHERPA)

- Electronic Theses
- Theses Alive!

These projects sowed the seed for much of the later work related to institutional repositories in the UK. For instance, staff at Edinburgh University were involved in the Theses Alive project which then resulted in the Edinburgh Research Archive (http://www.era.lib.ed.ac.uk/) and also in a book (Jones et al., 2006). The SHERPA/RoMEO project has developed into a partnership of some 33 institutions, all research-led institutions and all with practical exper ien ce of buildin g and populating e-print repositories. The information relating to publishers' policies on self-archiving maintained by SHERPA/ RoMEO , as shown in Figure 1.4, can be used by anyone throughout the world.

Digital Repositories Programme 2005-7

The aim of this programme was to continue the work started under FAIR and "to bring together people and practices from across various domains (research, learning, information services, institutional policy, management and administration, records management, and so on) to ensure the maximum degree of coordination in the development of digital repositories, in terms of their technical and social (including business) aspects". (http://www.jisc.ac.uk/whatwedo/ programmes/digital repositories 2005.aspx). There were some 30 projects funded during this 3-year programme – some built on earlier work (e.g. SHERPA) and others (e.g the EThOS project for a system of UK-wide electr on ic th eses deposit) covered newer ground.

Repositories and Preservation Programme 2007-9

The aim of this programme, which comes to an end in March 2009, is to "fund initiatives to develop the Information Environment supporting digital repositories and preservation, in cluding cross-searching facilities across repositories; funding for institutions to develop a critical mass of content, preservation solutions and advice for the development of repositories" (http://www.jisc.ac.uk/ whatwedo/programmes/reppres.aspx). There is a very large number of separate projects funded under this £14m. programme – almost 90. Examples of some of the projects are:

- Bradford University repository project (BURP)
- Federated Access to Repositories (FAR)
- KULTUR – a consortium to create a transferable and sustainable institutional repository model for research output in the creative and applied arts.

Repository Support Project (RSP)

The RSP is one of the many projects funded as part of the Research and Preservation programme. It has been a 2.5 year project to "co-ordinate and deliver good practice and practical advice to English and Welsh higher education institutions to enable the implementation, management and development of digital institutional repositories" (http://www.jisc.ac.uk/whatwedo/programmes/reppres/repsupport.aspx). As with many of the JISC-funded projects it has involved a consortium including staff from Nottingham University, Southampton University, UKOLN at Bath University as well as Aberystwyth University.

The opening page of th e RSP website (http://www.rsp.ac.uk) is shown in Figure 13 where it can be seen (down the left hand side) that there are links to many sources of information to assist anyone throughout the world who is involved in developing an institutional repository. These are being used. For instance, the Digital Repository Federation of Japan has translated the RSP planning checklists into Japanese.

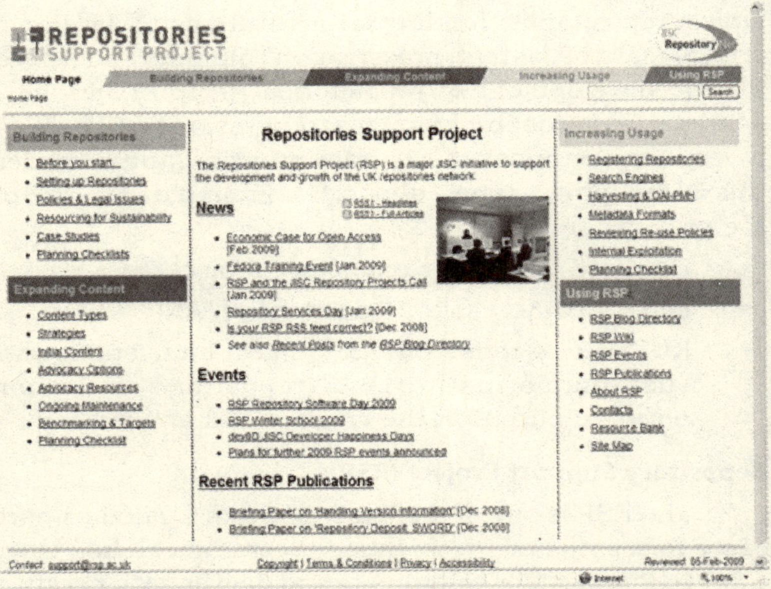

Fig. 1.13. Opening page of the RSP website

Welsh Repository Network (WRN)

The WRN is another project that has been funded by JISC under the Repositories and Preservation Programme. It has been run by Aberystwyth University, on behalf of WHELF (Wales Higher Education Libraries Forum), and aims to put in place an essential building block for the development of an integrated network of institutional digital repositories in one region of the UK – the country of Wales. At the start of the project in 2006 just two (Aberystwyth and Cardiff) of the higher education institutions in Wales had institutional repositories - and they were still operating as pilot projects. The WRN will be launched in February 2009 and staff from Aberystwyth have provided help, training and advice, using materials developed as part of RSP, for the participating institutions. In addition money has been available for the acquisition of appropriate hardware and software to support the development of the individual repositories. Although

Aberystwyth uses DSpace for its CADAIR repository individual institutions were free to choose their own software – one chose Eprints, one BEPress and the others chose DSpace. Various presentations on the work of the WRN, and Aberystwyth's work on the RSP, are available via CADAIR.

ACADEMIC STAFF AND INSTITUTIONAL REPOSITORIES: SOME PERSONAL EXPERIENCES

In 2004 there was a presentation at the National Library of Wales of some of the projects from the JISC-funded FAIR programme and this alerted me to the whole area of institutional repositories. In my department I thus became one of the early adopters of Aberystwyth's IR, CADAIR, when it was piloted by Information Services staff as part of the JISC-funded Repository Bridge project (Bell and Lewis, 2006). I have since been involved in attempting to help and encourage colleagues to deposit material. This has not been easy. As well as issues related to copyright aspects and the legal issues academics are not always able to retrieve the final 'post-print' version of a paper as accepted for publication. In the RSP documentation on Making a case for a repository some of the advantages for researchers are highlighted and these include:

- Increased visibility of research output and consequently the department and the institution
- Potentially increased impact of the research
- Help in managing and storing digital content connected with the research, including the underlying research data
- Help in managing the likely requirements of funding bodies for publications to be made available in a repository.
- Provides the possibility to standardise institutional records
- Allows the creation of personalised publications lists

- Offers usage metrics to determine hit rates on specific papers.

Looking at the statistics of use (as shown in Figure 14 for CADAIR) might encourage academics to deposit material – especially if impact of research becomes a key factor in research assessment procedures.

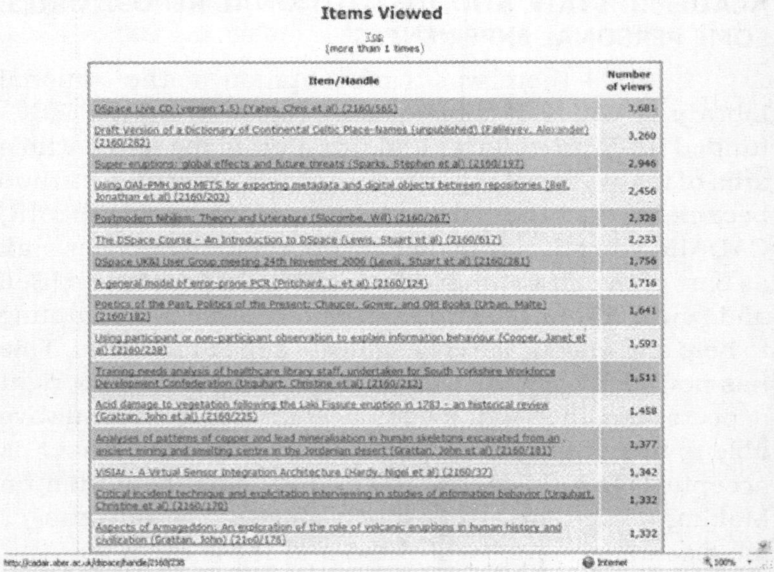

Items Viewed

Top
(more than 1 times)

Item/Handle	Number of views
DSpace Live CD (version 1.5) (Yates, Chris et al) (2160/565)	3,681
Draft Version of a Dictionary of Continental Celtic Place-Names (unpublished) (Falileyev, Alexander) (2160/282)	3,260
Super-eruptions: global effects and future threats (Sparks, Stephen et al) (2160/197)	2,946
Using OAI-PMH and METS for exporting metadata and digital objects between repositories (Bell, Jonathan et al) (2160/203)	2,456
Postmodern Nihilism: Theory and Literature (Slocombe, Will) (2160/267)	2,328
The DSpace Course - An Introduction to DSpace (Lewis, Stuart et al) (2160/617)	2,233
DSpace UK&I User Group meeting 24th November 2006 (Lewis, Stuart et al) (2160/281)	1,756
A general model of error-prone PCR (Pritchard, L. et al) (2160/124)	1,716
Poetics of the Past, Politics of the Present: Chaucer, Gower, and Old Books (Urban, Malte) (2160/182)	1,641
Using participant or non-participant observation to explain information behaviour (Cooper, Janet et al) (2160/238)	1,593
Training needs analysis of healthcare library staff, undertaken for South Yorkshire Workforce Development Confederation (Urquhart, Christine et al) (2160/212)	1,511
Acid damage to vegetation following the Laki Fissure eruption in 1783 - an historical review (Grattan, John et al) (2160/225)	1,458
Analyses of patterns of copper and lead mineralisation in human skeletons excavated from an ancient mining and smelting centre in the Jordanian desert (Grattan, John et al) (2160/181)	1,377
VISIAr - A Virtual Sensor Integration Architecture (Hardy, Nigel et al) (2160/37)	1,342
Critical incident technique and explicitation interviewing in studies of information behavior (Urquhart, Christine et al) (2160/170)	1,332
Aspects of Armageddon: An exploration of the role of volcanic eruptions in human history and civilization (Grattan, John) (2160/176)	1,332

Fig. 1.14. Statistics on use of materials in CADAIR

A full-time Repository Manager for CADAIR has been in place since September 2007 and one role of this person has been to talk to staff in individual departments to encourage use. There is much advice for repository managers wishing to promote and populate their repositories on the RSP website (e.g. http://www.rsp.ac.uk/pubs/briefingpapers- docs/repoadmin-promotion.pdf). In 2008 there was a major Research Assessment Exercise affecting all universities in the UK and a decision was made in Aberystwyth to include the metadata for all items submitted to the RAE to be included on CADAIR.

In 2008 Aberystwyth University mandated that all doctoral theses and masters dissertations gaining distinction be deposited in CADAIR. At a research school for masters students held in early February in my department the Repository Manager came to talk to students about CADAIR and the requirement for their dissertations to be submitted electronically. Academic staff supervising master's and doctoral students will need to ensure the appropriate copyright compliance in the work of their students with the outcomes being available electronically.

CONCLUSION

Although it is 18 years since the setting up of the Arxivdigital repository, and 16 years since Harnad's original proposal for open access it is really only in the last few years that there have been major developments in the area of open access and institutional repositories. This has come about from the mandates decreed by various funding institutions as well as individual universities and departments. As a result many institutions around the world are now involved in developing their own repositories. As Oppenheim (2008) concludes "we can expect funders to continue to move towards requiring OA outputs from the recipients of their funding, and institutions to move steadily towards mandating OA. It will be an interesting time."

REFERENCES

Association of Research Libraries. (2009). The research library's role in digital repository services. Washington DC; Association of Research Libraries. Retrieved from http://www.arl.org/bm~doc/r epository- services-report.pdf

Bailey, Charles W., Institutional repositories: Tout de suite. Digital Scholarship. Retrieved from h ttp://www.dspace.org/images/LinkTo/irtoutsuite.pdf

Bell, J. and Lewis, S. (2006). Using OAI-PMH and METS for exporting metadata and digital objects between repositories, Program: *Electronic Library and Information Systems*, 40(3), pp.268-276. Retrieved from http://cadair.aber.ac.uk/dspace/handle/2160/203.

Fernandez, Leila. (2006). Open access initiatives in India: an evaluation. Partnership: *The Canadian Journal of Library and Information Practice and Research*, 1(1). Retrieved from http://journal.lib.uoguelph.ca/index.php/perj/article/view/110/171

Harnad, S. (1995). A subversive proposal. In: Okerson, A. and O'Donnell, J. (eds.) Scholarly Journals at the Crossroads: A Subversive Proposal for Electronic Publishing. Washington DC; Association of Research Libraries. Retrieved from http://www.ecs.soton.ac.uk/~harnad/subvert.html

Heery, R. and Anderson, S. (2005). Digital Repositories Review, UKOLN and AHDS. Retrieved from http://www.jisc.ac.uk/uploadeddocuments/digital-repositories-review-2005.pdf

Jenkins, Celia., Probets, Steve., Oppenheim, Charles and Hubbard, Bill. (2007). RoMEO Studies8: Self-archiving: The logic behind the colour-coding used in the Copyright Knowledge Bank. Program: *Electronic Library and Information Systems*, 41(2) pp.124-133.

Joint Information Systems Committee. (2006). Open access briefing paper No. 2. Retrieved from *http://www.jisc.ac.uk/publications/publications/pub_openaccess_v2.aspxhttp://journal.lib.uoguelph.ca/index.php/perj/article/view/110/171*

Jones, R., Andrew, T. and McColl, J. (2006). The institutional repository. Oxford, Chandos.

Lynch, C. A. (2003). Institutional Repositories: Essential Infrastructure for Scholarship in the Digital Age. ARL: A Bimonthly Report, No.226 (February 2003). Retrieved from http://www.arl.org/resources/pubs/br/br226/br226ir.shtml

Mittal, Rekha and Mahesh, G. (2008). Digital libraries and repositories in India: An evaluative study. Program: *Electronic Library and Information Systems*, 42(3) pp.286-302.

Oppenheim, Charles. (2008). Electronic scholarly publishing and open access. *Journal of Information Science*, 34(4), pp.577-590.

Simpson, Pauline. (2006). Repositories for research: Southampton's evolving role in the knowledge cycle, Program: *Electronic Library and Information Systems*, 40(3), pp.224-231.

2

Establishing Institutional Repositories: An overview

Usha Mujoo Munshi

INTRODUCTION

Over the past few years Institutional Repository (IR) has emerged as a novel scholarly publishing and communication model. An IR is also sometimes called as an e-print archive. An IR is digital archive of the research output of faculty, research staff, and student of a university, academic and R&D institution and usually accessible freely to end users both within and outside of the university/institution. An IR is also viewed as a set of services that a university or an institution offers to the members of its community for the management and dissemination of digital materials created by members of the community. IR could include research material such as the following:

- Published material (e.g. journal papers, book chapters, and conference papers),
- Unpublished/gray research material (e.g. pre-prints, working papers, theses and dissertations, technical reports, project reports, and learning material); and

- Supporting research material (e.g. data sets, models, and simulations).
- Any other type of resources specific to the given institution or organizations.

IRs work alongside existing publishing system, play a supplementary role. They take advantage of the digital networked medium in overcoming some of the limitations of current system and bring several significant additional benefits to the scholarly community and to the agencies that fund, support and manage research.

RELEVANCE OF INSTITUTIONAL REPOSITORIES

IRs along with open access journals (journals accessible by users and libraries without charge), are viewed as key approaches to overcome two key problem prevailing in the current scholarly publishing model very high subscription cost of commercial and many society journals, coupled with static/ dwindling library budgets and the restrictions imposed by publishers for accessing e-versions using various digital rights management schemes (example, ILL using e-versions is not allowed). An organization's IR enables the organization to capture, preserve and provide (with some exceptions) free online access to intellectual assets produced by the organizations community. This results in wider access, improved usage and impact of organizations research. There is growing evidence that freely accessible online material is used and cited more compared to online material having restricted access.

Further, IRs enhance research capacity of our researchers by providing opportunity for more local research material to be accessible worldwide such as working papers, theses, technical reports, paper published in Indian journals and conferences. By enabling increased re-use of organizations/ university's intellectual assets, IRs contribute to increased return on investment of research.

BENEFITS OF INSTITUTIONAL REPOSITORIES : INSTITUTIONAL & INDIVIDUAL LEVEL

IRs brings specific benefit to institution and individual researchers.

Institutional level

Benefits at institutional level include:

- Showcase institutional research by bringing it together in one place which otherwise is distributed over several publishing channels;
- Demonstrate the quality, and scientific, social and economic relevance of an institutions research;
- Increase the institutions visibility, status and public value;
- Facilitate improved research knowledge management, including research monitoring and assessment.

Individual Level

Benefits IRs brings to individual researchers include:

- Establish priority for their research finding (made possible by date stamping and publication identifier);
- Provide wider access and visibility to their research publications and thereby improve impact
- Global level cross archive search services bring additional visibility to local research publication, globally.
- Share unpublished ideas and know-how's with their peers and obtain their feedback; and
- Support long-term preservation of their research papers (even beyond their tenure)

More importantly, IRs are an organizational level response to support faculty seeking innovative approaches to research dissemination which otherwise they would have tended to explore and experiment on their own, for example through their home pages.

Further, most IR software today comply with international metadata standard and interoperability protocols. These have enabled development of global level cross-archive search services and provide access to content aggregated from different IRs. This brings additional visibility to local research publications.

FEATURES AND FUNCTIONALITY OF INSTITUTIONAL REPOSITORY

IRs share several common features and functions. Key common features include:

- IR contains digital content (born-digital or digitized) and this could be in various forms such as text, images, audio, video, and data sets;
- IR is community-driven, members typically belonging to an institution or consortium;
- Members of the community also are the authors and copyright owners of the content;
- IR has institutional support and commitment;
- IR provides durable and permanent access to deposited documents; and
- With some exceptions, an IR provides open access to its content, to both internal and external users.

Increasingly, an additional feature expected of an IR is that it should be interoperable, requiring it to expose its metadata as per the OAI-PMH protocol for developing cross-archive aggregation and search services.

In addition to these core features, an IR also supports several specific functions. These include:

- Registration of institutional users (authors) for document submission and other privileged use;
- Document submission, including user

authentication, metadata assignment, license approval and document uploading;

- Approval/ moderation of submitted documents, including metadata and format approval and peer review;
- Archiving, including date stamping, identifier assignment, preservation support, indexing and storage;
- Dissemination, including provision of search and browse front-end, OAI registration and compliance and rights management; and
- Administration, including definition and management of document formats,
- Metadata, licenses, and submission policies.

SETTING UP AN INSTITUTIONAL REPOSITORY: REQUIREMENTS AND PROCESSES

A checklist of processes related to planning, implementing and maintaining an IR is provided in Annexure-I. Typically, the organization's/ university library has the main responsibility for setting up and maintaining the IR and to provide related services. It could take help from the organizations computer center/ IT department for installing and configuring required hardware and software, if such expertise is not available within the library. Setting up and managing an IR is a serious, long term undertaking. It is useful to appoint an IR Manager who is responsible for the IR, on behalf of the Librarian. Other tasks that will require, typically, part time in nature, personnel support are: user support, advocacy, training and proxy/ mediated submissions.

Infrastructure

Setting up an IR and provision of services require suitable IT and network infrastructure, including server computer hardware and software, campus-wide LAN (intranet) and Internet connectivity

Software -Institutional Repositories

The vista of software platforms for building institutional repositories is constantly in a flux of change. Fortunately a wide options of open source IR software is available today free of cost (http://www.soros.org/openaccess/software). A list of open source softwares is also annexed as Annexure II.

Some of the commonly used institutional repository software platforms with few examples are listed below:

Greenstone

Greenstone (http://www.greenstone.org/cgi-bin/library) is free multi-lingual, open source software developed by the New Zealand Digital Library Project at the University of Waikato. Greenstone is a suite of software for building and distributing digital library collections. Greenstone was developed and distributed in cooperation with UNESCO and the Human Info NGO. Examples include: New Zealand Digital Library

http://nzdl.sadl.uleth.ca/cgi-bin/library Indian Institute of Management, Kozhikodehttp://www.iimk.ac.in/gsdl/cgi-bin/library .

DSpace

Dspace (http://www.dspace.org) is free, open source software jointly developed by MIT and Hewlet Packed Labs. Dspace is digital library system designed to capture, store, index, preserve, and redistributes the intellectual output of a university's research faculty in digital formats. Examples include: Massachusetts Institute of Technology (MIT) https://dspace.mit.edu/, Documentation Research & Training Centre (DRTC) https://drtc.isibang.ac.in/.

EPrints

GNU EPrints (http:/software.eprints.org) is free, open source software developed at the University of

Southampton. It is designed to create a pre-print institutional repository for scholarly research, but can be used for other purpose. Examples include: University of Southampton, UK [http://eprints.soton.ac.uk/], Indian Institute of Science (IISc), Bangalore [http://eprints.iisc.ernet.in/].

CDSware (CERN Document Server Software)

CDSware (http://cdsware.cern.ch) is free, open source software developed by CERN, the European Organization for Nuclear Research, based in Geneva. CDSware is designed to run an electronic preprint server, online library catalogue, or a document system on the web.

Fedora (Flexible Extensible Digital Object Repository)

Fedora (http://www.fedora.info/index.shtml) is free, open source software jointly developed by University of Virginia and Cornell University. Fedora serves as foundation for building interoperable web-based digital Libraries, institutional repositories, and other information management systems. It demonstrates how you can deploy a distributed digital library architecture using web-based technologies, including XML and Web services. Example includes : University of Queensland, Australia http://espace.library.uq.edu.au/

Bepress

Bepress (http://www.bepress.com/repositories.html) is commercial software developed by the Berkeley Electronic Press. Bepress builds and hosts their customers repositories. Cost includes software, custom implementation, infrastructure, training, hosting, offsite backup, technical support, and software upgrades.

CONTENTdm(DiMeMa)

CONTENTdm (http://contentdm.com/) is commercial software developed at the University of

Washington, & is distributed by OCLC. In August 2006 OCLC acquired DiMeMa, developer of software for digital media management. CONTENTdm Digital Collection Management is a tool for providing everything from organizing and managing to publishing and searching digital collections over the Internet. It also offers scalable tools for archiving collections of any size. Example includes: University of Washington http://content.lib.washington.edu/ ; Alaska's Virtual Library and Digital Archives

VITAL

VITAL (http://www.vtls.com.products/vital.shtml) is commercial software, product of VTLS. VITAL is an institutional repository solution designed for universities, libraries, museums, archives and information centers. This software is designed to simplify the development of digital object repositories and to provide seamless online search and retrieval of information for administrative staff, contributing faculty and end users. Example includes: Australian Research Repositories Online to the World http://www.arrow.edu.au/

ECONOMICS OF INSTITUTIONAL REPOSITORIES

Following is a break up of cost components involved in setting up and maintaining an IR:

Start-up costs

- Hardware (IR server, backup facility, network connectivity)
- Software (free, if open source)
- Installation and customization
- Policies and procedures

Ongoing costs

- Advocacy- getting content
- Support- IR hardware and software, user support

- Mediated submission
- Upgrade/ migrations

Long-term costs

- Digital Preservation

Considerable attention and continuous effort will be needed to obtain and retain the support of organizations/ university administrators and faculty/ academic/research community for the implementation and maintenance of the IR; and to reduce or remove resistance these people may feel towards the IR and have them cooperate/ participate actively.

INSTITUTIONAL REPOSITORY: PLANNING, IMPLEMENTATION AND EXECUTION

While conceiving a plan for the IR, thorough understanding and utmost care needs to be taken. The planning for setting up of an Institutional repository needs through understanding and analysis of the resources and the nature of its contents, which the IR is going to contain. There are various tasks involved to initiate, implement and in making the repository operational. Broadly these tasks can be grouped under four following areas of activity:

I. Orientation Phase

II. Planning Phase

III. Implementation Phase

IV. Operational/ Maintenance Phase

The tasks to be performed under these four areas are given in the Annexure I. Though the guidelines given in Annexure I are not detailed ones, yet the checklist can be used for developing one.

CHANGE AGENTS INSTITUTIONAL REPOSITORIES

Growing understanding that knowledge produced by publicly funded research a global public good, needs to be shared, fuelled the current rapid growth of Open Access Archives (OAA). Growth is also due to the adoption of common technical standards defined by the OAI & common protocols for retrieving metadata, enabling distributed OAI-compliant archives to be searched seamlessly. Geographical location of a paper in an OAI-compliant archive has no effect on the ability of Search Engine such as OAIster & Google to find it.

The real change agents are the Open Access Initiatives. The brain starter step regarding Open Access Initiative was the Budapest one, after which several steps took place.

Budapest Open Access Initiative: The Budapest Open Access Initiative arose from a small but lively meeting convened in Budapest by the Open Society Institute (OSI) on December 1-2, 2001. The purpose of the meeting was to accelerate progress in the international effort to make research articles in all academic fields freely available on the internet. http://www.soros.org/openaccess/index.shtml . The initiative was launched in February 2002.

The following are important initiatives to support the open access movement which have occurred since the launch of the BOAI in February 2002:

- Association of College & Research Libraries (ACRL) Principles and Strategies for the Reform of Scholarly Communication, August 28, 2003 http://www.ala.org
- Bethesda Statement on Open Access Publishing, June 20, 2003 *http://www.earlham.edu/~peters*
- Berlin Declaration on Open Access to Knowledge in the Sciences and Humanities, October 22, 2003 *http://www.zim.mpg.de/openaccess-berlin*
- UN World Summit on the Information Society Declaration of Principles and Plan of Action, December 12, 2003 *http://www.itu.int - Document*

1; http://www.itu.int - Document 2

- Organisation for Economic Co-operation and Development (OECD) Declaration on Access to Research Data From Public Funding, January 30, 2004. *http://www.oecd.org*
- The International Federation of Library Associations and Institutions (IFLA) released the IFLA Statement on Open Access to Scholarly Literature and Research Documentation, February 24, 2004. *http://www.ifla.org*

INSTITUTIONAL REPOSITORY DEVELOPMENT

Global IR development

Worldwide several organizations/ universities have already set up IRs. It is estimated that there are over 350 such repositories in universities. You can have lot of information regarding various facets of repositories at *http://www.sherpa.ac.uk/index.html.* Also OpenDOAR - a directory of worldwide open access repositories can be accessed at *http://www.sherpa.ac.uk/projects/opendoar.html.* A few examples include:

- Australia National University (*http://eprints.anu.edu.au/*)
- University of Waikato : The New Zealand Digital Library (*http://nzdl.sadl.uleth.ca/cgi-bin/library*)
- University of Montreal (Canada) (*http://papyrus.bib.umontreal.ca/*)
- University of Essen (Germany) (*http://miless.uni-essen.de/*)
- Queensland University of Technology (Australia) (*http://eprints.qut.edu.au/*)
- CERN scientific information service (*http://cds.cern.ch/*)
- University of Glasgow (UK) (*http://eprints.lib.gla.ac.uk/*)

- University of Nottingham (UK) (*http://eprints.nottingham.ac.uk/*)
- Caltech (USA) (*http://coda.caltech.edu/*)
- MIT (USA) *http://hpds1.mit.edu/index.jsp*)
- Others

Information about such OAI-compliant repositories worldwide is available at several open archives registries, including the Open Archives and Eprints registries.(*http://www.openarchives.org/*, *http://archives.eprints.org/*) . You can also get a selective country wise list at *http://www.opendoar.org/countrylist.php* .

Apart from such institutional level efforts, several national level initiatives have been launched recently in Netherlands (DARE- The Digital Academic Research), UK(FAIR- Focus on Academic Institutional Resources), Australia and South Africa, to promote and support coordinated development of IRs in these countries.

NATIONAL ENDEAVOURS

Several initiatives taken up by various organizations to set up IRs . Mention may be made of some of these repositories.

ePrints@IISc (*http://eprints.iisc.ernet.in/*), the e-prints archive of the Indian Institute of Science, Bangalore, is the first OAI-compliant academic IR to be set up in India (late 2002). *e-journal@insa* portal launched for public consumption in late 2002 facilitates unlimited, unrestricted and free access to all its research journals published since 1930's. Several other institutional repositories are out there. Thanks to a series of workshops and training programmes conducted since then by agencies like INSA, DRTC, NCSI, MSSRF and others. Due to these forums, several more IRs has recently been set up.

Table 2.1. Institutional Repository Initiatives in India

Name of IR institution	*Website address*	*Software used*
Association of Indian Labour Historians, Delhi	*http://www.indialabourarchives.org/home.htm*	Greenstone
DRTC, ISIBangalore	*http://drtc.isibang.ac.in*	DSpace
IIM, Kozhikode	*http://www.iimk.ac.in/gsdl/cgi-bin/library*	Greenstone
IISc, Bangalore	*http://etd.ncsi.iisc.ernet.in/*	DSpace
IISc, Bangalore	*http://eprints.iisc.ernet.in/*	EPrints
IIT, Bombay	*http://www.library.iitb.ac.in/~mnj/gsdl/cgi-bin/library*	Greenstone
IIT, Delhi	*http://eprint.iitd.ac.in/dspace/*	DSpace
INFLIBNET, Ahmedabad	*http://dspace.inflibnet.ac.in*	DSpace
INSA, Delhi	*http://www.insaindia.org/informatics_centre/service.htm*	DSpace
National Chemical Laboratory	*http://dspace.ncl.res.in*	DSpace
National Informatics Centre	*http://openmed.nic.in*	EPrints
NIT, Rourkela	*http://dspace.nitrkl.ac.in/dspace*	DSpace
IIT, Kharagpur	*http://www.dspace.iitkgp.ernet.in; http://www.library.iitkgp.ernet.in/usr/elib/digital.htm*	DSpace

IMPETUS FOR INSTITUTIONAL REPOSITORY DEVELOPMENT

At global and national level, impetus and support for developing IRs is coming from different quarters. Several recent developments seem to augur well for more intensive growth of IRs. These include:

- UK Science and Technology Committee Inquiry: Scientific Publications: Free for all? (July 2004) strongly recommends that all UK higher education institutions establish institutional repositories on which their published output can be stored and from which it can be read, free of charge, online. It also recommends that Research Councils and other

Government funders mandate their funded researchers to deposit a copy of all of their articles in this way.

- U.S. House Appropriations Committee, concerned by insufficient public access to reports and data resulting from NIH-funded research, recommends that any manuscript resulting from NIH research support, be deposited in the PubMedCentral (PMC) research repository, enabling free access.
- Similar requirement by funding agencies like OECD, Howard Hughes (USA), and Wellcome Trust (UK)
- Scholarly Publishing and Resources Coalition (SPARC, USA)- development s of guidelines, supporting materials and resources for setting up IRs
- Budapest Open Access initiative (BOAI) Golden (open access journals) and Green (self archiving in IRs) path to open access
- Open Society Institute(OSI)- by supporting workshops, training programmes and resources material for setting up IRs
- Growing number of publishers permitting pre-print/ post print archiving of journal papers
- Growing number of publishers permitting authors to retain copyright of their publications, but license of publisher to first sale rights

SIGNIFICANCE OF INSTITUTIONAL REPOSITORY TO INDIAN ACADEMIC & RESEARCH ORGANIZATIONS

There is significant opportunity for developing a network of inter-operable IRs in India, given the large number of public supported universities, institutions of higher learning and research laboratories in the country. Government ministries and departments in the country support a very large number of R&D labs in various sectors (industrial, defense, agriculture, medical, biotechnology, environment, S&T, IT, space, energy, ocean development, etc.). In the academic sector there are close to 300 universities and institutions of higher learning, supported by MHRD and UGC.

These organizations produce significant number of research-based publications, including technical reports, working papers, patents, theses, manuals, learning material, etc., apart from pre-prints and post-prints of papers in refereed journals and conferences. These publications constitute the key research output and in many ways the intellectual property of these organizations. Only a very small portion of this research gets published in formal medium like journals and conferences, which again has limited access due to publisher restrictions. A network of inter-operable IRs will go a long way in improved access, sharing and re-use of this research output.

Strategies for Institutional Repository Development with Special Reference to Indian Institutions of Higher Learning.

Development and deployment of interoperable IRs in Indian institutions of higher learning will require initiatives and actions by different agencies at various levels. Organizations like INSA, IISc. Bangalore, ISI-DRTC, M.S. Swaminathan Research Foundation and others actively supported and promoted culture of creation of IRs and propagated open access culture. While INSA is a signatory to Berlin Declaration, supports open access movement, through various forums. Following several workshops focusing an open access to scholarly communications and institutional repositories by various organizations like INSA (first seminar on open access organized in the country inviting leading speakers from world including CODATA- President) set the tone for spreading the word and building Institutional Repositories. However since then number of training programs/ workshops/seminars has set the ball further rolling. Mention may here be made of DRTC, ISI ; M.S. Swaminathan Research Foundation, IISc, Bangalore with special reference to NCSI training programs on Institutional repositories. Several institutions have since initiated the process and set up IRs, and a few more institutions are in process of setting up their IRs. However more concerted and coordinated effort is required by various bodies such as MHRD and UGC to get all the universities and institutions of higher learning to establish their IRs. To achieve maximum effectiveness, coordination with other Government departments like DST and some key agencies such as Science Academies like INSA, New Delhi and IAS, Bangalore will be needed to evolve a nation-wide initiative. A policy and action level plan however should be prepared before proceeding with implementation nation-wide.

Much of the recommendations made by the UK Science and Technology Committee Inquiry: *Scientific Publications: Free for all?* (July 2004) related to open access in general and IRs in particular are worth considering by Indian agencies (e.g.; MHRD, UGC, Science Academies, etc), while evolving a plan for deployment of IRs in academic institutions in the country. Lessons learnt and experiences from National level initiatives in other countries which are at advanced stage of formulation/ implementation, for example UK, Netherlands and Australia, also needs to be taken into consideration. This will help in evolving systems that are customized to meet our specific needs and are also compatible globally.

INSTITUTIONAL REPOSITORY RESOURCES

Following is a list of core literature and resources related to IR.

- The Case for Institutional Repositories: A SPARC position paper. Release 1.0, 2002. http://www.arl.org/sparc/IR/ir.html
- SPARC Institutional Repository checklist & resource

guide. Release 1.0, Nov 2002. http://www.arl.org/sparc/IR/IR_Guide.html

- Clifford A. Lynch Institutional repositories: Essential infrastructure for scholarship in the digital age. ARL Bimonthly Report 226, February 2003 http://www.arl.org/newsltr/226/ir.html
- Susan Gibbons. Establishing an institutional repository. *Library Technology Reports.* Vol. 4, No. 4 July/ August 2004.
- Publisher and Library /Learning Solutions (PALS) Pathfinder Research on Web based Repositories. Final Report, Mark Ware Consulting Ltd., UK. January 2004. http://www.palsgroup.org.uk/palsweb/palsweb.nsf
- SPARC Institutional Repositories List. A select list of institutional repositories around the world. http://www.arl.org/sparc/core/index.asp?page=m1
- The Open Society Institute (OSI). The guide of Institutional Repositories Software. 2nd ed. January 2004. http://www.soros.org/openaccess/software

Further Information

- The Continuing Access and Digital Preservation Strategy for the Joint Information Systems Committee (JISC) 2002 http://www.jisc.ac.uk/index.cfm?name=pres_continuing
- JISC Digital Repositories Programme: http://www.jisc.ac.uk/index.cfm?name= programme_digital_repositories
- Day, Michael, 2003, Collecting and Preserving the World Wide Web: a feasibility study undertaken for JISC and the Wellcome Trust: http://www.jisc.ac.uk/uploaded_documents/archiving_feasibility.pdf
- Jones, Maggie, 2003, Archiving E-Journals

Consultancy - Final Report: http://www.jisc.ac.uk/uploaded_documents/ejournalsfinal.pdf

- The Digital Creation Centre: http://www.dcc.ac.uk
- JISC Briefing Paper on Digital Repositories: http://www.jisc.ac.uk/index.cfm?name=pub_repositories
- Lord, Philip, and Macdonald, Alison, 2003, Data curation for e-Science in the UK: an audit to establish requirements for future curation and provision http://www.jisc.ac.uk/uploaded_documents/e-ScienceReportFinal.pdf 15.
- James, Hamish, et al, 2003, Feasibility and Requirements Study on Preservation of E-Prints http://www.jisc.ac.uk/uploaded_documents/e-prints_report_final.pdf
- Wheatley, Paul, 2003, Survey and assessment of sources of information on file formats and software documentation: http://www.jisc.ac.uk/uploaded_documents/FileFormatsreport.pdf
- Circular 9/02: Supporting Institutional Records Management (closed) http://www.jisc.ac.uk/index.cfm?name=programme_supporting_irm18
- Supporting Digital Preservation and Asset Management in Institutions http://www.jisc.ac.uk/index.cfm?name=programme_404

ANNEXURE 2.1

INSTITUTIONAL REPOSITORIES: CHECKLIST FOR PLANNING, IMPLEMENTATION AND OPERATION

Phase No.	*Task No*	*Phase and related tasks*
I		**Orientation Phase**
	1	Understand the what and why of IR. Be able to articulate the features, functionality and benefits of IR Study model IRs their content, features and services.
II		**Planning Phase**
	1.	Establish local aims for the IR
	2.	Fix Principles and Policies that relates to fundamental basis upon which your IR depends & determine the nature of our IR
	3.	Provide strategic direction for IR -subject to minimal change over time
	4.	Decide on in house implementation and maintenance or outsourcing (e.g. consortia-level repository)
	5.	Make a survey of stakeholders, (lack of) support and resistance; make a plan to continually gain support and deal with the resistance
	6.	Assess resource requirements and costs involved in the IR implementation and maintenance
	7.	Decide on your copyright policies for objects in the IR, including approvals to be taken from authors and publishers. Draft/use standardized agreements for content providers
	8.	Decide on centralized and /or decentralized submission, and on level of support from the Library/IR-staff
	9.	Decide on type of objects to be included, including teaching objects, level (full file and metadata always or metadata only if full file not available), quality criteria for objects (formal and w.r.t. content), and on access control (protection of sensitive research results). Think also of student (students these) and independent researchers
	10.	Decide on permitted object formats for all objects in the IR
	11.	Decide on user groups/communities, e.g. department, lab, research centre
	12.	Decide on work flow and responsibilities Review of quality/ appropriateness of submission, metadata review, archiving

13. Decide on policy for inclusion of metadata per object type and quality level, as far as possible in relation to any services to be developed
14. Decide on the (limits of the) responsibilities of the IR Manager
15. Allocate other technical and non-technical manpower
16. Decide classification of authorization and access levels, depending on quality criteria
17. Decide local policy on long term preservation and preservation period
18. Decide output demands, hardcopy, softcopy
19. Choose IR software
20. Specify IR server and network connectivity requirements

III Implementation Phase

1. Draw up implementation plan
2. Work out processes or procedures that are beneficial or prudent, that facilitate successful operation of IR and may change as environment changes.
3. Draw up a communication/promotional plan, to address resistance among academics who may fear that the IR will hinder their publication chances in a regular journal. SPARC calls this a briefing paper
4. Set up project website for IR. Use this project website also for (the development of) the documentation.
5. Find early adopters and start filling/building the IR with this group
6. Map (volume of) local academic output
7. Select objects for initial filling of IR
8. Allocate manpower with appropriate skills for technical installation (once-only) and for operation and maintenance after installation
9. Strain people for technical installation and maintenance
10. Allocate hardware and network resources
11. First installation and test of the bare system
12. Customize and configure IR
13. Initial input content, experimentation and move to production service
14. Certify for OAI compatibility

IV Operational/Maintenance Phase

1. Draw up operational/administrative/maintenance procedures

2. Make available for harvesting and services
3. Increase, monitor, promote continuous input
4. Produce reports, including access log analysis
5. Continuous communication with authors and users
6. Evaluate and analyze effects
7. Continue populating the repository
8. Ensure regular IR content backup
9. Handle IR software and hardware upgrades
10. Subscribe to IR software mailing list

Note: *based on a checklist drawn for the Dutch DARE programme (www.surf.nl/DARE) (contact: Ms.Lilian van der Vaart (e-mail: vaart@eleftheria.demon.nl), with some enhancements by (Late) DR. T.B. Rahashekar, NCSI, IISc and Usha Mujoo Munshi (e-mail: umunshi@isical.ac.in)*

ANNEXURE 2.2

SOME POPULAR OSS

Name of software	*Developer*	*Web Address*	*License*	*System requirements*	*Operating System*
CDSWare Server	CERN Document	*http://cdsware.cern.ch*	GNU General Public License	MySQL database server and Apache/ {PHP, Python}	Unix
Dspace	Massachusetts Institute of Technology (MIT) libraries and Hewlett-Packard labs	*http://www.dspace.org*	BSD License	Apache web sever, Tomcat servlet engine and the postgre SQL relational database system	Unix or Linux
E-prints	University of Southampton	*http://sofware.eprints.org/*	GNU General Public License	Apache, MySQL database, Perl Language	Unix
Fedora Universities	Virginia and Cornell	*http://www.fedora.info*	Mozilla Public License	Sun java Software, MySQL /Oracle 9	Windows Unix
Greenstone	University of Waikato, UNESCO and the human Info (NGO)	*www.greenstone.org*	GNU General Public License	Apache Web Server, MySQL Database, Perl Language	Windows, Linux/ Unix
i-Tor	NIWI-KNAW	*www.i-Tor.org/en/system_info/about*	GNU General Public License	Java script, MySQL Jetly web server	Unix / Linux
iVia	INFOMINE, LOOK, MEL & Virtual reference lib.	*http://infomine.ucr.edu/ivia/ivia.php*	AGPL(13) Free Software License	MySQL & Berkeley DB Management Packages, C++	Linux

phronesis	CONACYT, ITESM	*http://copernico.mty.itesm.mx/phronesis/project*	GNU General Public License	————	Unix , Linux
ROADS	Inst. of Learn. & Res. Tech. (ILRT) UK Office of Lib. & Infor. Networking	*http://www.ukoln.ac.uk*	Artistic License GNU/ GPL	HTTP Apache web server & Perl language	Unix

3

Developments of Institutional Repositories: An Overview

Jayaprakash

Digital Library is where the past meets the present and creates the future...

Dr. A.P.J. Abdul Kalam
Former President of India

INTRODUCTION

Libraries are heart of the organizations due to their information resources, and librarians are knowledge administrators who know the importance of information, knowledge transfer and resource sharing. On the other hand, Technology has become a significant change agent in all aspects of our lives. Now, we are more aware of how we communicate, how we share, how we interact with people, and how we learn. IT is useful in most stages of the knowledge sharing process, and it is used for content management. Internet, IT, and ICT developments have facilitated resource sharing activities. Advent of ICT has opened up new opportunities for proper mutual cooperation among libraries.

It is well recognized that libraries all over the world

are undergoing transformation, especially owing to the development in information and communication technologies. Traditional libraries are changing to digital libraries and new libraries that are being set up are increasingly of the digital kind. As a result, there is widespread interest and consequently, a lot of research and development activities are being carried out in this area all over the world. Libraries are today playing a lead role in the creation of institutional repositories supporting the cause of open access.

An Institutional repository is a digital archive of the intellectual output of an Institution. It makes the quality of scholarship produced at that Institution accessible to others worldwide over the Internet.

IRs will have two common characteristics:

Heterogeneous data formats : Although the primary target will be refereed research papers, content need not be limited to this type of content: for example, data and correspondence supplementing published results are likely to start appearing with greater use of IRs by authors.

Low cost per item deposited : IRs must keep costs low enough not to jeopardize open access.

There is a tendency among those working in the field to treat digital preservation as a primary concern.

CHALLENGES AND OPPORTUNITIES IN CREATING DIGITAL REPOSITORIES

Following are the challenges and opportunities one would face while building institutional repositories;

- Building digital collections of national importance from existing texts, documents, images etc.
- Creating new digital documents and linking them
- Subject portals: Selecting and maintaining open source digital resources.

- Developing /adapting management tools for digital collections
- Providing access to digital collections
- Integrating digital & other library collections (Arora, Jagadish, n.d.)

IR DEVELOPMENTS AT THE INTERNATIONAL LEVEL

WSIS Declaration of Principles and Plan of Action

The United Nations-backed World Summit on the Information Society (WSIS) strongly supported open access to information and knowledge (United Nations, 2005). This confirms that member countries of the United Nations will take appropriate strategic decisions to bring scholarly literature, produced from public funded research initiatives or state-supported researchers, under the umbrella of open access. In this instrument, some specific principles and plan of action were suggested relevant to digital preservation of cultural contents, creation of local contents and open access to scholarly literature.

UNESCO Universal Declaration on Cultural Diversity

The United Nations-backed Universal Declaration on Cultural Diversity strongly promotes the concept of digitizing documentary heritage collections for initiating intercultural dialogue which is the best guarantee of peace (UNESCO, 2001). This Declaration confirms that member countries of the United Nations will take appropriate strategic steps to bring cross-cultural documentary heritage collections accessible to worldwide communities.

Open Access Statements and Declarations

In the wake of the open access movement, some policy frameworks have already been established by member communities to foster inclusive, plural and development-oriented knowledge societies. A number of open access declarations/ statements were made during the past decade, where the world's leading research institutions agreed on the open access mandates.

Hyderabad Declaration, 2004

The ICT Ministers in the Asian Region met in Hyderabad in the *Asia IT Ministers' Second Summit* during 12-13 January 2004 and adopted a collective principle of undertaking definitive and firm steps to spread the benefits of ICT. In this declaration, digitization of culture is one of the bold provisions to spread the benefits of ICT to the common citizens.

NATIONAL POLICY

NKC Recommendations on Libraries and Open Educational Resources

The National Knowledge Commission of India (NKC), constituted on 13th June 2005, is a high-level advisory body to the Prime Minister of India, with a mandate to guide policy and direct reforms. NKC's overarching aim is to transform India into a vibrant knowledge-based society. The NKC's *Working Group on Libraries* and *Working Group on Open Access and Open Educational Resources* have strongly recommended digitization of documentary heritage collections, open access to public-funded research literature and supported establishment of open courseware repositories for countrywide dissemination of quality courseware to many cross sections of people. If implemented, these recommendations will have far-reaching implications in the knowledge creation and dissemination cycle.

The documentary heritage collections, scholarly literature and lifelong learning materials digitized or produced by state-sponsored institutions would then be made accessible through open access channels such as national and institutional repositories. This way the NKC's recommendation on peer-reviewed research papers resulting from public-funded research would be validated by subject experts when making these resources available through open access channels. NKC also recommended creation of national knowledge portals for basic needs/ key sectors such as water, energy, environment, education, food, health, agriculture, employment and citizen rights. Already national portals on water (India Water Portal, www.indiawaterportal.org), energy (India Energy

Portal, www.indiaenergyportal.org), environment (India Environment Portal www. Indiaenvironment portal.org.in) and education (Sakshat, *www.sakshat.ac.in*) have been launched that provide open access to information, knowledge and learning resources on the relevant areas. An excerpt of relevant recommendations and open access statements of NKC (2006, 2007) is highlighted below:

Summary of NKC Recommendations to Prime Minister of India *on Libraries (2006)*

Set up a National Commission on Libraries.

- Prepare a national census of all libraries Revamp library information science (LIS) education, training and research facilities.
- Re-assess staffing of libraries.
- Set up a central library fund.
- Modernize library management, encourage greater community participation in library management.
- Promote information and communication technology (ICT) applications in all libraries.
- Facilitate donation and maintenance of private collections.
- Encourage public private partnerships in LIS development.

On Open Educational Resources (2007)

- Support the production of quality content by a select set of Indian institutions.
- Leverage global open educational resources.
- Encourage open access.
- Develop network-enabled delivery infrastructure.
- Create a faculty and institutional development programme.

On Other Thrust Areas – having relevance on Open Access

- Protection of traditional knowledge (TK) through Traditional Knowledge Digital Library (TKDL) and promoting incentives for wealth creation from TK [Intellectual Property Rights, 2007]
- Set up a National Education Foundation to develop web-based common open resources [Open and Distance Education, 2007]

UGC (SUBMISSION OF METADATA AND FULL-TEXT OF DOCTORAL THESES IN ELECTRONIC FORMAT) REGULATIONS, 2005

In 2005, the University Grants Commission of India (UGC) drafted a national policy framework entitled "UGC (Submission of Metadata and Full-text of Doctoral Theses in Electronic Format) Regulations, 2005". This Regulation proposed two sets of planned actions such as:

- Creation of Indian National Theses Database (INTED).
- Submission of PhD Theses in Electronic Form.

This set of regulations is still under consideration. They propose to formulate a roadmap to achieve widest dissemination of results of doctoral research conducted in Indian universities and bibliographic control of theses and dissertations of research degrees. So far, a few UGC-supported universities have established open access repositories for scholarly literature produced in the respective universities. Initially the universities were reluctant to change their status quo, as the contents of scholarly literature including the PhD theses will be a matter of critical analysis by the national and international peers, if the universities establish open access repositories. Now, universities will be motivated to produce qualitative doctoral theses and will maintain certain international standards.

The UGC also supports development of infrastructure in Indian universities through various planned schemes. The proposed national education grid will also enrich modern ICT infrastructure in Indian universities. The Indian universities then will have necessary infrastructure to host a number of Web-based information services. Hosting an ETD repository and providing online interface to INTED will not be a problem in most of the universities. Indian universities should now take a proactive role in the implementation of these regulations at the earliest, ensure qualitative research and make the results of doctoral research widely available. The UGC should also clear all bottlenecks to implement INTED and decentralized ETD repositories across the country.

Benefits of Institutional Repositories are:

- Improved visibility and impact-Institutional, National;
- Contribute to institutional knowledge management;
- Improve Research collaboration-interdependent, inter-Institutional, International;
- Enhanced status and reputation;
- Enhanced research capacity.

CONCLUSION

Institutional repositories (IRs) have become a hot topic over the last few years, and many institutions around the world are actively considering or working towards implementing them. The IR is a very powerful tool that can serve as an engine of information transfer. It has been recognized as an essential infrastructure of scholarly information dissemination. The IR provides a method for capturing and maintaining today's electronic detritus so that tomorrow's scholars can understand the thinking behind the published record. For the standard IRs, each and every institution should have to equip its library professionals so that they are able to cope up with the ever-growing changes in this part.

REFERENCES

Arora, Jagdish (n. d.), Digital Libraries Initiatives in India Concepts, Cases and Emerging Issues at www.dyuthi.cusat.ac.in/xmlui/bitstream/handle/purl/.../DLIMMNEW.PPT

Bhat, M. H.(2010). Open access repositories: A review. *Library Philosophy and Practice,* 1-8.

Biradar, B. S., & Banteppanavar, K. (2013). Steps of developing digital repository using dspace: An experience of Kuvempu University. *DESIDOC Journal of Library and Information Technology, 33* (6), 474-479.

Brown, A. (2015). Automating preservation: New developments in the PRONOM service. *RLG DigiNews, 9* (2).

Heidari, A., & Khakpour, A. (2013). Practical experiences of resource sharing activities in the Islamic Consultative Assembly Library (ICAL) . *IFLA WLIC 2013.* Singapore.

Patel, Y., & V. J. (2005). Institutional digital repositories/e-archives: INFLIBNET's initiative in India. In M. G. Sreekumar (Ed.), *7th MANLIBNET Annual National Convention* (pp. 312-318). Calicut: ESS ESS.

Philip, L., & Macdonald, A. (n.d.). *e-Science Curation Report.* Retrieved from Data Curation for e-Science in the UK: An audit to establish requirements for future curation and provision JISC: *http://www.jisc.ac.uk/uploaded documents/e-ScienceReportFinal.pdf.*

Shukla, V.N (n.d.). Digitization practices in India: Issues and challenges. Retrieved from www.delnet.nic.in/dlindia.ppt

4

New Metrics of Scholarly Communication and Emerging Roles of Academic Librarians: A Case of Institutional Repositories

Priti Jain

INTRODUCTION

New metrics of scholarly communication and digital scholarship have emerged primarily, owing to advanced development of Information and Communication Technologies (ICTs).Scholarly Communication is the process of conducting research and sharing the results from creation to dissemination and preservation of knowledge for teaching, research, and scholarship (Purdue University Libraries, 2015). The evolution of digital infrastructures has challenged the traditional scholarly communication system. Digital Scholarship (DS) and openness are the latest trends of making research publications freely available. OA is a paradigm shift from the traditional model of scholarly communication to open access.

There are two majorstrategies to Open Access: Open Access publishing in Journals (Gold Route)and Open Access Self-Archiving in repositories(Green Route).The "golden road" of OA journal publishing is where journals provide OA to their articles (either by charging the author-institution for refereeing/publishing outgoing articles instead of charging the user-institution for accessing incoming articles, or by simply making their online edition free for all). The "green road" of OA self-archiving is where authors provide OA to their own published articles, by making their own e-prints free for all. Providing gold OA is in the hands of publishers while green OA is in the hands of researchers (Harnad, 2012). "The idea of an IR comes with the idea of open access to overcome the cost factors and information communication barriers of reaching, displaying and communicating research directly to large audiences while removing intermediaries"(Nagra, 2012:138).

Open Access repositories are digital collections that make their contents freely available over the Internet. These digital repositories collect the research output of the members of a university's research community and support the archiving and long-term preservation of the institution's intellectual output (Swan & Chan 2009). Bjork, et al. (2013:3) define OA repository as "a repository with a wide range of scholarly materials including, e-prints and electronic dissertations and theses (EDTs) that are made available on the Internet free either in the institutional repositories, or subject specific repositories or personal web pages". Through OA repositories authors provide open access to their research-outputs by making them free to everyone.

There are four types of repository publications: the subject-based repository, the research repository, the national repository system and the institutional repository (Jain, 2012). The focus of this paper is academic institutional repositories. IRs are usually hosted within academic libraries to digitally collect and preserve academic papers and documents in order to make them freely accessible to the students, faculty and the public and IRs are transforming librarians' roles and benefitting librarians in numerous ways such as providing opportunities for increased visibility and institutional presence, and working hand-in-hand with academia. In the above background, this paper discusses Institutional Repositories as New Metrics of Scholarly Communication and evolving roles of academic librarians.

The terms Institutional Repositories (IRs) would refer to repositories in academic institutions through-out the paper. Academic librarians are defined as those librarians, who have library qualification and work in higher education institutional libraries including either college or University. Since, IRs are Green Routes to OA, thesetwo terms IRs and OA are sometimes used interchangeably in the paper.

AIM & OBJECTIVES

The main aim of this paper is to discuss institutional repositories as new metrics of scholarly communication and digital scholarship with focus on emerging roles of academic librarians. The paper is organized in the following main sections:

- Benefits of IRs;
- Potential Impediments to IR success;
- IR as a benchmark of Digital Scholarship;
- Emerging Roles of Academic Librarians in IR; and,
- Conclusion and recommendation

METHODOLOGY

This paper is based on in-depth desk-top review of relevant literature and the author's own points of view.

INSTITUTIONAL REPOSITORIES (IRs) DEFINED

IR has been defined diversely by different authors. Johnson (2002) defines an IR as a digital archive of the intellectual product created by the faculty, research staff, and students of an institution and accessible to end-users both within and outside of the institution with few if any barriers to access.

According to the most frequently cited IR definition from Lynch (2003), IR is: [. . .] a set of services that a university offers to the members of its community for the management and dissemination of digital materials created by the institution and its community members. It is most essentially an organizational commitment to the stewardship of these digital materials, including long-term preservation where appropriate, as well as organization and access or distribution. This definition valuably formalizes the concept of stewardship, service provision and commitment and describes IR appropriately.

Shearer (2013) has aptly articulated the characteristics of an IR:

- An IR is digital; it collects digital material only.
- An IR is institutionally defined because it represents the intellectual outputs of a particular institution.
- An IR collects only scholarly contents.
- It is cumulative and perpetual; because once submitted material cannot be withdrawn from an IR and all materials keep accumulating for a long term preservation and accessibility.
- An IR is Open Access because it provides free and open access to its contents.
- An IR is interoperable; because its metadata can be harvested and all the documents can then be jointly searched and retrieved as if they were in one global collection, accessible to everyone (Open Archives

Initiative 2002). Another type of IR interoperability is integration of the IR with course management tools (Crow, 2002; Lynch, 2003; Jain & Bentley, 2008; Shearer, 2013).

BENEFITS OF IRs

Literature review reveals several benefits of IR, which can be grouped into the following main categories:

Benefits to the Institutions

According to Pickton and Barwick (2006) for an institution, an IR is:

- A means of increasing global visibility and prestige of the institution; it may be used to support marketing activities to attract high quality staff, students and funding;
- A supporting tool for learning and teaching;
- IR is an instrument to standardise institutional records;
- A way of breaking down publishers' costs and permissions barriers;
- An alleviation of the requirement to trust publishers to maintain information in the long term;
- A instrument to long-term digital preservation of institutional intellectual outputs;
- A single consolidated integrated system; research outputs are usually located in different information systems and users have difficulty in searching, browsing and accessing the scattered information and there is no systematic way to deposit all types of scholarly output of the institution in digital format such as, conference papers and technical reports, unpublished literature. An IR provides a single consolidated, integrated system for easy access (Farida, Tjakraatmadja, Firman & Basuki, 2014).
- A mechanism to keep track of and analyse research

performance; some institutional repositories are integrated with faculty profile tools that showcase individual researchers, their research interests, and their publications, which and can help departments manage and track their publishing output (Palmer, 2014).

- A medium to keep academic community up to date. "By establishing flourishing repositories, faculty, researchers, and institutions keep up with the latest scholarly communication trends. It increases their participation and role in the research and communication process, as well as increases their visibility and value to the community" (Pickton & Barwick, 2006; CARL & SPARC, 2008;Jain, 2011; Nagra, 2012;Palmer, 2014).

Benefits to Authors

According to Pickton & Barwick (2006).An IR offers:

- More exposure and universal access of research work; repositories make authors' work available to everyone. By increased research dissemination there is high impact of scholarship publications with the high citation rate. Also, "Research is more valuable when it is shared. It enables new research to build on earlier findings. It is not only fuelling further advancement of knowledge, it brings scientists and scholars the recognition that advances their careers" (CARL & SPARC, 2008:2) and as a result, IR scholarly works are accessible to world-wide audiences (Farida, Tjakraatmadja, Firman & Basuki, 2014).
- A platform for the storage and access to a wide range of material;
- Greater security and longer term accessibility of research outputs compared to a personal web site;
- Feedback and commentary; through IR, authors are

able to assert priority and receive commentary on pre-publication 'pre-prints';

- Added value services such as hit counts on papers, personalised publication lists and citation analyses, linked CVs;
- A central archive of a researcher's work (Pickton & Barwick, 2006;CARL& SPARC, 2008; Jain & Bentley, 2008;Jain, 2011; Nagra, 2012).

Benefits to Students

CARL and SPARC (2008) reported that IR offers benefits to students. For instance,no library can afford to subscribe to all the resources students need, hence; through a digital/institutional repository students can read and learn from them. Also, students benefit from digital repositories by depositing their theses and dissertations expanding the accessibility of these important works (CARL & SPARC, 2008).

Benefits to Librarians/libraries

IR provides the following benefits and opportunities to academic librarians:

- Increased visibility and institutional presence; academic librarians become visible institution-wide through IRs because most IRs are owned by librarians. By virtue of their expertise to own and manage IRs librarians are much esteemed by the academic institution and thus they improve their image.
- Opportunity to work with academia; IRs create avenues that enhance cross-fertilization of ideas among scholars. Through IRs academic librarians work with academia as intellectual property and copyrights advisors and facilitate self-archiving.
- Viable partner in research; According to an empirical study in United States carried-out by Rieh, et al

(2007), IRs provide libraries with the opportunities to develop new strategies and standards for digital collection management and have even expanded the perception of the library as a "viable research partner" in institutions. The study established that library's role as a viable research partner made the biggest jump, with almost 50% respondents acknowledge library's role as a viable partner in the research.

- IR is a means to provide improved services to library customers; through the establishment of IRs libraries have minimized serial and permission crises. This enhances library customer services and consequently, customer satisfaction.
- Opportunity to lead IR projects based on their inherent skills; it exposes academic librarians to IRs training and on-job experience. Hence, it gives opportunity to librarians to showcase their inherent skills in IR project
- IRs are time-effective for both librarians and students in searching for scholarly materials on line.

In summary, the primary benefit of institutional repositories is that they raise the visibility and enhance the accessibility of publications by providing free, unrestricted, online access to these publications (Palmer, 2014:24). The potential uses of an IR are for: scholarly communication; management and storage of learning materials, electronic publications and research collections; preservation of digital research work; building university profile by showcasing academic research work; providing an institutional leadership role for the library; research assessment; encouraging open access; and housing digitised collections (Barton & Waters, 2004).

POTENTIAL IMPEDIMENTS TO IR SUCCESS

Despite numerous benefits, there are potential

impediments to IR success. Pickton & Barwick (2006) identify the following impediments to IRs:

Cost : Due to freely available open source software the initial financial cost for IR is not high, but the on-going maintenance costs may be significant.

Sustaining support and commitment : Often, it is difficult to sustain continuous support and commitment from the management and academic staff. Lynch (2003) has succinctly described this obstacle: "Stewardship is easy and inexpensive to claim; it is expensive and difficult to honour, and perhaps it will prove to be all too easy to later abdicate". Hence, there is a need for institutions to think seriously before launching institutional repository programs, and not merely 'jump on the band wagon'.

Rights management issues : Sometimes researchers are apprehensive about infringing publisher copyright and lack adequate awareness about their own intellectual property rights. They may be dubious in the case of preprints about making their work available online before it is published by a traditional publisher.

Working Culture issues : Contributing content to user-generated or 'self-service' sites is perceived as time-consuming by hard pressed academics. They may be happy to contribute content but reluctant to do it themselves. This necessitates mediated deposit services.

Policy Issues : An IR will only function to its optimal potential when a mandate is in place to populate it. Otherwise, researchers can react negatively to any suggestion of compulsion. Policies developed to monitor quality of submissions also serve as constrains however quality assurance is important to some administrators. Lynch (2003) cautioned that an IR should not become a tool for enforcing administrative control over academic work.

Lack of incentives : In the absence of any incentive academics feel reluctant to provide even bibliographic details of their scholarly output especially when they know that incentives are available in other institutions.

Content Recruitment : It is difficult to grow a repository when researchers lack the motivation to deposit, overestimate the time and effort required, are overwhelmed by the complexity of copyright issues (Palmer, 2014).

Complexity of new scholarly communication models : present noteworthy challenges for academic libraries (Cassidy, et al, 2014).

In spite of the above mentioned challenges, the biggest challenge in implementing an IR remains the promotion of the benefits it offers, whilst allaying stakeholder concerns since IRs are still new to some of the academic world, particularly in developing countries.

CURRENT STATUS OF IR WORLD-WIDE

There are total 2989 institutional repositories world-wide. The following Figure 4.1 displays the current repositories around the world.

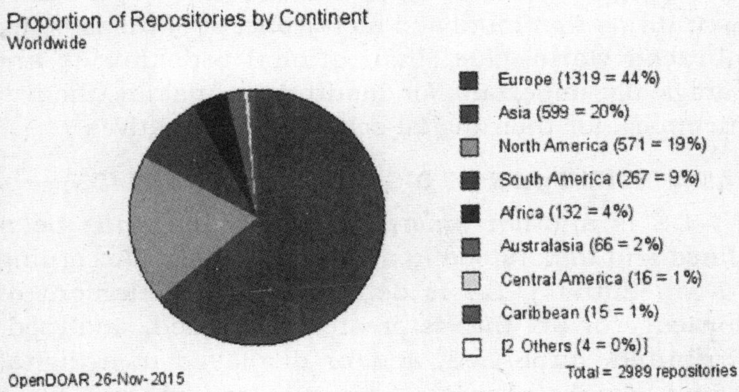

Fig. 4.1. Proportion of Repositories by Continent - Worldwide (*Source* : OpenDOAR, 2015).

According to the Figure 4.1, there are total of 2989 institutional repositories around the world, of which 1319 are in Europe, 599 in Asia, 571 in North America, 267 in South America, 132 in Africa, 66 in Australasia, 16 in Central America and 15 belongs to Caribbean (OpenDOAR 2015).

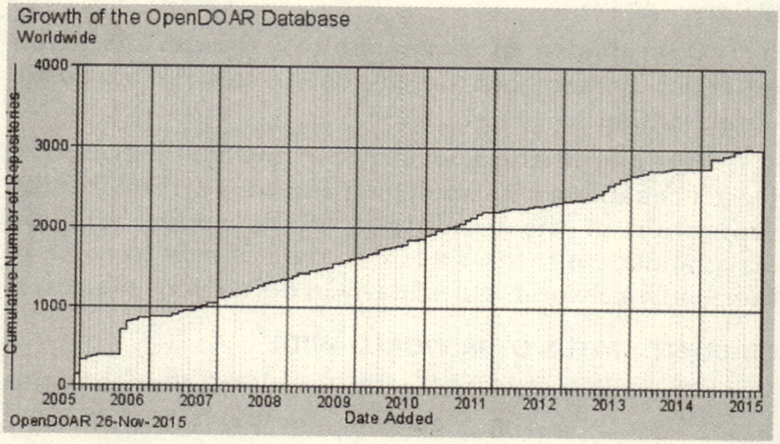

Fig. 4.2. Growth of the Open DOAR Database - Worldwide

In Figure 4.2, the significant and steady growth of IRs confirms that more and more concept of IRs is being embraced world-wide. Institutional repositories are strategically important for institutions making them a benchmark for their digital scholarship initiatives

IR AS A BENCHMARK OF DIGITAL SCHOLARSHIP (DS)

DS is another emerging area, which has been defined and understood in a number of ways. According to Foot (2007:1), DS is defined as, "any element of knowledge or art that is created, produced, analyzed, distributed, published, and/or displayed in a digital medium, for the purpose of research or teaching". On a similar note, a Digital Publishing Librarian at Ohio State University defines DS as "research and teaching that is made possible by digital technologies, or that takes advantage of them to ask and answer questions in new ways" (Sinclair, 2014:1). The above two definitions do not seem to capture the totality of digital activities in any tertiary institution. Therefore DS can be defined as an integrated collaborative combined environment which embraces cutting-edge technologies in learning, teaching, research, professional and administrative services (Task Group on UB and Digital Scholarship, 2008).

According to American Council of Learned Society (2006), "digital scholarship" has meant several related things:

- Building a digital collection of information for further study and analysis
- Creating appropriate tools for collection-building
- Creating appropriate tools for the analysis and study of collections
- Using digital collections and analytical tools to generate new intellectual products
- Creating authoring tools for these new intellectual products, either in traditional forms or in digital form.

An IR comprises all the above characteristics and sits firmly within the DS landscape. A most-cited and well-recognised IR proponent Lynch (2003) strongly regards institutional repositories as essential infrastructure for scholarship by arguing that "the development of institutional repositories emerged as a new strategy that allows universities to apply serious, systematic leverage to accelerate changes taking place in scholarship and scholarly communication". Markey et al (2007:1) further deliberate, that "a considerable portion of the scholarly record is born digital, and some scholarship is produced in digital formats that have no physical, in-the-hand counterparts. The proliferation of digital scholarship raises serious and pressing issues about how to organize, access, and preserve it in perpetuity". According to Markey et al (2007), academic institutions have built and deployed institutional repositories (IRs) to manage the digital scholarship of their learning communities. This seems to suggest that achieving the realisable success of digital scholarship can depend on the success of the institutional repository.

An IR is dynamic in all respects and it satisfies every element of digital scholarship characteristics. IRs are a strong infrastructure component of a research data management and data sharing strategy, as they are designed to easily store data files that support scholarly publications (Palmer, 2014). IR is a concept that looks at managing digital data of all sorts both for now and the future; it will evolve along with the whole digital scholarship environment and even foster and catalyse developments.

The currency of an IR is another benchmark of Digital Scholarship. In Indonesia Open Access Institutional Repositories (OAIRs) are knowledge management initiative and IR objective is not only to preserve, organize, and disseminate the local content of campus community, but also to enhance visibility of higher education scholarship. There are 35 Indonesian OAIRs that appear in the Repository World Web, which shows that Indonesian higher education OAIR has a competitive position among world repositories (Farida, Tjakraatmadja, Firman & Basuki, 2014). IR administrators promote IR, outreach, train, supervise, perform quality control, manage metadata and provide customer service, which in turn allow them to cultivate and disseminate scholarship produced at their institutions (Palmer, 2014). A strong Institutional Repository is a sign of a strong Digital Scholarship System; as they are open access platforms for scholarly communication to showcase and share scholarships digitally.

EMERGING ROLES OF ACADEMIC LIBRARIANS IN IR

Even the most well-endowed research library cannot afford to provide access to all of the content requested by its faculty and students and it is still worse in the developing world because of limited budgets. Hence, librarians have been amongst the most vocal advocates for open access showing their support for open access by signing on to open access initiatives and petitions and through their institutions or associations (Swan & Chan, 2014). An IR provides the platform to maximize collection and that is why academic libraries are increasingly building IRs.

IRs are transforming academic librarians' role in numerous ways. IRs prompt librarian to become proactive opposed to their traditional role of being reactive.To keep pace with the changing scholarly communication and digital scholarship, librarians are encouraged to become proactive by assisting faculty in producing their scholarly work. For instance, by observing production of research-outputs, academic librarians can assist in productions and ingestion processes (Walter, 2007) and also assists in submitting research outputs in IRs. Institutional repositories are transforming traditional reference librarians to modern reference librarians. According to Nixon (2002), "Reference librarians are a library's eyes and ears. They understand users' needs and perceptions. They know what's working and what's not. When they act as subject selectors, they are the library's primary liaison with faculty in their subject areas and its most visible representatives. They know how to help, inform, persuade, and teach users. For an IR to succeed, it is essential that reference librarians are involved in its planning, implementation, and operation." Bailey Jr. (2005) suggested several ways on how reference librarians can play a significant role in planning, establishing, and supporting IRs, for example, helping to create IR policies and procedures; assisting in designing the IR user interface so that it is clear and easy to use.

Academic librarians are re-emerging as content producers and disseminators as opposed to their traditional role of information managers by facilitating submission of research-outputs into IRs. Academic librarians are transforming from traditional information protectors to intellectual property right advisors and from traditional cataloguers to data managers and data curators. Librarians have critical roles to play in both establishing and maintaining an IR. Jain & Bentley (2008) have identified the following emerging roles of academic librarians:

Promote IR : Librarians can act as change agent by promoting IRs. For that reason, they need to know all about the IR, its principles, benefits and operational processes in order to promote it and act as 'IR evangelists' (Ashworth 2006). OA proponent Suber (2008) has proposed the following suggestion to promote OA:

- Launch an open-access, OAI-compliant institutional eprint archive, for both texts and data;
- Help faculty deposit their research articles in the institutional archive;
- Consider publishing an open-access journal;
- Undertake digitization, access, and preservation projects not only for faculty, but for local groups e.g. non-profits, community organizations museums, galleries, libraries.
- Join SPARC, a consortium of academic libraries actively promoting OA

Building content : Librarians can employ advocacy and marketing strategies to promote engagement with faculty members and help to generate IR contents. They can also assist by proactively searching for content independently (Jain & Bentley, 2008).

Collection administrators and metadata specialists : Librarians have potential roles as collection administrators and metadata specialists. For effective implementation of IR, libraries need to recruit or train librarians with digital collection management and who can provide a mediated deposit service for reluctant 'self-archivers' (Jain & Bentley, 2008). Institutional repository administrators do all this to cultivate and disseminate the scholarship at their institutions. They also respond to requests from academic departments to create new collections and reconfigure existing collections (Palmer, 2014).

Trainers : Librarians should be able to train staff and students to use the IR and help them prepare their digital products (Jain & Bentley, 2008).

Self-archiving facilitators : Most academic libraries are assuming leading roles in self-archiving their institutional outputs in digital repositories. Purdue libraries participate in a variety of research and engage in collaborative/interdisciplinary research by applying library science to other disciplinary problems. Purdue's e-Pubs, provide access to publications and other scholarly materials freely over the Internet; and, provides to its faculty members, students and researchers (Purdue University Libraries, 2015).

Consult on copyright issues : to determine if a paper, or given version of a paper, can be deposited (Palmer, 2014).

CHALLENGES SPECIFIC TO LIBRARIANS

Open Access Publishing has challenges that are specific to librarians. Academic librarians are constantly challenged to understand the concept of scholarly communication practices including scholars' use of prepublication research material that were not traditionally part of the library domain (Antelman, 2004). Librarians are continuously challenged to learn and adopt new technologies and new ways of scholarly communication and publication, such as metadata (Galligan, 2013). These new skills include communication skills, capabilities for OA and managing open access process. It also includes metadata and web scale, ability to be creative and even radical. All these skills play an essential role in explaining open access to researchers Libraries need to evolve as the needs arise and be prepared to be creative and adaptive as the researchers and students' access and use of information are changing and will continue to change (Harris, 2012). Librarian needs to advice researchers on various issues such as who pays for the article-processing charges, working with publishers in the new scholarly environment (Harris 2013).

Today there is growing number of open access sources, it is also a challenge for librarians to manage and maintain their collection in new digital and information environment.

Complexity of new scholarly communication and publishing models: present significant challenges fo academic libraries. Since information seekers can acces any types of information using world-wide web applications, modern librarians also advocate fo sustainable models of scholarly communication. Fo instance, ARL librarians and archivists are both avi consumers and creators of scholarship. They consum and disseminate research and best practices throug journal articles, conference papers.Also, they use a emerging technologies such as, ListServ, webinars, blogs Use Aids, and Social Media Websites, slide share podcasts to stay up-to-date on the profession's lates research (Cassidy, et al, 2014).

CONCLUSION

From the ongoing discourse, it is obvious that a IR satisfies digital scholarship characteristics a previously outlined: building digital collections, creating tools for collecting, analyzing, and authoring digital information; using digital collections and analytical tools to generate new intellectual products (American Council of Learned Society, 2006). It is a concept that looks at managing digital data of all types for both present and future. Despite numerous obstacles associated with IRs, it remains clear that organisations are increasingly realising both importance and added value benefits of IRs (MIRE, 2009). According to Basefsky (2009), IRs should serve as full-fledged electronic libraries and thereby serve the purpose of collecting, disseminating, analysing and exchanging useful digital information for academic purposes and should be coupled with full range of academic and research support services enabled by new technologies.

Steady growth of IRs clearly marks their place in the digital scholarship. It is also apparent that academic librarians have critical roles to play in the successful execution of IRs. However, the libraries need to make critical decisions and choices before designing or redesigning institutional repositories. Among them are the funding, staffing, technology, metadata, content and operations to build, manage and run the institutional repositories successfully (Nagra, 2012:137).

RECOMMENDATIONS

In order to make IR more successful, the following recommendations are put forward:

- A comprehensive promotion and publicity of the benefits of IR to the faculty and all other stakeholders by academic institutions, with librarians playing a central role in the comprehensive promotion. The OA advocacy should be accompanied by awareness campaigns.
- Formulation of clear vision, strategy and policies on ownership of research output, IR contents,

quality standards, intellectual property/copyright issues and other matters related to publishing open access research.

- Adoption of a strict institutional implementation policy to mandatory deposit ofall staff research outputs and students' dissertation and thesis;
- Consideration of IRs as ongoing projects not once done and dust;
- Sustainable support from the senior management and academia;
- Adequate provision of resources (finance, space, human and technology); and
- Introduction of incentives to encourage academia to publish through IRs and academic librarians to manage IR more seriously.

REFERENCES

American Council of Learned Societies. (2006). Our cultural commonwealth: The report of the American Council of Learned Societies Commission on cyber infrastructure for the humanities and social sciences. Retrieved from: *http://www.acls.org/uploadedFiles/Publications/Programs/Our_Cultural_Commonwealth.pdf.*

Antelman, K. (2004). Do open-access articles have a greater research impact? *College & Research Libraries,* 65(5), 372-382.

Bailey, Jr. C. W., (2005). The Role of Reference Librarians in institutional repositories. Retrieved from: *http://www.digital-scholarship.org/cwb/reflibir.pdf*

Barton, M. R & Waters, M. M. (2004). Creating an institutional repository: LEADIRS workbook.*MIT Libraries.* Retrieved from: *http://dspace.org/implement/leadirs.pdf*

Basefsky, S.M. (2009). The end of institutional repositories and the beginning of social academic research service: An enhanced role for libraries. Retrieved from: *http://digitalcommons.ilr.cornell.edu/cgi/viewcontent.cgi?article=1007&context=conference.*

Bjork, B.C., Roos, A. & Lauri, M. (2009). Scientific journal publishing: yearly volume and open access availability. *Information Research,* 14(1).Retrieved from: *http://informationr.net/ir/14-1/paper391.html.*

CARL & SPARC. (2008). Greater reach for your research: Expanding readership through digital repositories. Retrieved from: *http://www.carlabrc.ca/uploads/pdfs/sparc_repositories.pdf.*

Cassidy, R.S. et al. (2014). Beyond gatekeepers of knowledge: Scholarly communication practices of Academic Librarians and Archivists at ARL Institutions. *College & Research Libraries,* 75(2), 145-166.

Crow, R. (2002). *The Case for Institutional Repositories: a SPARC Position Paper.* Retrieved from: *http://www.arl.org/sparc/bm~doc/ir_final_release_102.pdf*

Farida, I. et al. (2014). A conceptual model of open access institutional repository in Indonesia academic libraries: Viewed from knowledge management perspective, *Library Management,* 36(1/2), 168 – 181. Retrieved from: *http://www.emeraldinsight.com/doi/abs/10.1108/LM-03-2014-0038.*

Foot, K. (2007). Digital scholarship colloquium. Retrieved from: *http://www.rch.uky.edu/DSC/DSCI/DSCposter.pdf.*

Galligan, G. (2013). Open access metadata: challenges for libraries and a big solution. Retrieved from: *http://www.swets.com/blog/open-access-metadata-challenges-for-libraries-and-a-big-solution#.VCqdbxbCdVI.*

Harnad, S. (2012). What is open access? Retrieved from: *http://www.eprints.org/openaccess/*

Harris, S. (2012). Moving towards an open access future: The role of academic libraries.Retrieved from: *http://www.uk.sagepub.com/repository/binaries/pdf/Library-OAReport.pdf.*

Harris, S. (2013). Implementing open access APCs: The role of academic libraries. Retrieved from: *http://www.uk.sagepub.com/repository/binaries/pdf/apc.pdf.*

Jain, Priti & Bentley, Gemma. (2008). Institutional repositories as a benchmark for digital scholarship. Paper presented at the Botswana Library Association 1st National Conference held at University of Botswana Library Auditorium, Gaborone, Botswana, 26th - 28th June 2008. ISBN: 99912-573-7-3, 116-130.

Jain, Priti. (2011). New trends and future applications/directions of institutional repositories in academic institutions, *Library Review*, 60(2), 125-141.Retrieved from: *http://www.emeraldinsight.com/journals.htm?issn=0024-2535&volume=60&issue=2.*

Jain, Priti. (2012). Promoting open access to research in Academic libraries: Development and Initiatives. *Library Philosophy and Practice.* May 2012 Issue, ISSN 1522-0222, Retrieved from: *http://www.webpages.uidaho.edu/~mbolin/jain.pdf*

Lynch, C. (2003). Institutional repositories: Essential infrastructure for scholarship in the digital age. *ARL*, 226, 1–7.Retrieved from: *http://www.arl.org/bm~doc/br226ir.pdf.*

Markey, K. et al. (2007). Census of Institutional Repositories in the United States. Retrieved From*http://www.google.co.bw/search?hl=en&q=Markey+2007+Council+on+Library+and+Information+ Resources+% 2B+institutional+repository&btnG=Search&meta.*

MIRE (2009). The institutional repository in 2010 ... and beyond. Retrieved from: *https://atmire.com/presentations/OnlineInformation2009/Repositories-in-2010.pdf*

Nagra, K.A. (2012). Building institutional repositories in the academic libraries. *Community & Junior College Libraries*, 18(3-4), 137-150.

Nixon, W. J. (2002). The evolution of an institutional e-prints archive at the University of Glasgow, *Ariadne*, 32.Retrieved from: *http://www.ariadne.ac.uk/issue32/eprint-archives/.*

OpenDOAR (2015). Directory of open access repositories. Retrieved from: *http://www.opendoar.org/*

Open Archives Initiative. (2002). The Open Archives Initiative Protocol for Metadata Harvesting version 2.0. Retrieved from: *http://www.openarchives.org/OAI/openarchivesprotocol.htm*

Palmer, L. A. (2014). Cultivating scholarship: The role of institutional repositories in health sciences libraries. *Against the Grain*, Retrieved from: *http://escholarship.umassmed.edu/cgi/viewcontent.cgi?article=1157&context=lib_articles*

Purdue University Libraries.(2015). Scholarly communication at Purdue.Retrieved from: *https://www.lib.purdue.edu/scholarlyComm*

Rieh, S.Y. et al. (2007). Perceived Values and Benefits of Institutional Repositories: A Perspective of Digital Curation. Retrieved from: *http://www.ils.unc.edu/digccurr2007/papers/rieh_paper_6-2.pdf*

Shearer, K. (2013). Institutional Repositories: Towards the identification of critical success factors. Retrieved from: *http://www.caisacsi.ca/ojs/index.php/cais/article/download/408/578*

Sinclair, B. (2014). The university library as incubator for digital scholarship.Retrieved from: *http://www.educause.edu/ero/article/university-library-incubator-digital-scholarship.*

Suber, P. (2008). What librarians can do to promote open access? Retrieved from: *http://library.uncw.edu/uploads/pdfs/OpenAccessLibrarians.pdf.*

Swan, A. & Chan, L. (2009).Support and implementation of open access.Retrieved from: *http://www.openoasis.org/index.php?option=com_content&view=article&id=136&catid=79&Itemid=258.*

Swan, A. & Chan, L. (2014).Why librarians should be concerned with open access. Retrieved from:*http://www.openoasis.org/index.php%3Foption%3Dcom_content%26view%3Darticle%26id%3D254%26Itemid%3D256.*

Task Group on UB and Digital Scholarship. (2008). Final report of the task group on UB and digital scholarship, University of Botswana, Gaborone.

Walter, T.O. (2007). The new academic library-building institutional repositories to support changing scholarly and research processes. Retrieved from: *http://www.ala.org/acrl/sites/ala.org.acrl/files/content/conferences/confsandpreconfs/national/baltimore/papers/56.pdf*

5

Institutional Digital Repositories : A platform to promote the Visibility & Impact of Institutional Research

Sobhagyawati Gupta

INTRODUCTION

Today we are living in the age of Information Revolution. There have been a lot of changes in library and information activities in the world. The changes in the late 90s and thereafter have been very fast. Old technologies of information exchange are being replaced by new technologies and methods. Basically two fundamental changes have been observed by the library: (i) The abundance of the digital resources and (ii) Development of ICTs. The demands of information users and researchers are increasing day-by-day. The old information delivery and seeking methods are being replaced by applying new modified technology-based methods.

In this age, internet become an essential medium for information exchange and with its help anyone can communicate his/her information with another at anywhere in the world to maintain scholarly communication. The tremendous growth of Internet and WWW, high resolution capture devices, highly capacity digital storage media, multi-faceted search engines, fast processing power of computer, dropping computer cost and increased bandwidth network have forced librarians and information professionals to integrate them and develop new methods, like open access, digital publishing and self archiving and academic digital repositories. It's new technique for digital collage building, managing preserving information and crating new information in digital form in institution and about institution, access to preserve and use information and as well as content submission and organization of information. Institutional repositories are an emerging trend among institutions of higher education as a tool to make knowledge bank of an institution's intellectual output to the global community via the Internet. By this way, the academic institutions are performing their social obligation to disseminate their research output to a larger audience. An institutional repository (IR) is a digital collection of a university's scholarly and creative output. IR is a part of larger global information system of repositories providing the foundation for a new model of scholarly publishing.

INSTITUTIONAL REPOSITORY (IR)

Repository means formally organized and managed collection of digital content generated by faculty, staff and students of an institution. The main purpose of institutional repositories is to bring together and preserve the intellectual output of the academic community. IR is a set of services that an institute offers to the members of its community for the management and dissemination of digital materials created by the institution and its community. IR may contain the intellectual works of faculty and students – both research and teaching material and also documentation of the activities of the institution itself in the form of records of events and performance and of the ongoing intellectual life of the institution. IR may also contain experimental and observational data captured by members that supports scholarly activities and to preserve them and make them available to the members of their communities and to the public.

According to the SPAR, an IR is 'a digital archive of the research output of faculty, researchers, and students of an institution and usually accessible freely to end users both within and outside of the institution'. It is supported by a set of information technologies, but an important part is services that comprise the management of technological changes, and the migration of digital content from one set of technologies to the next as part of the organizational commitment to providing repository services.

ESSENTIAL ELEMENTS OF IR

A digital institutional repository could be any collection of digital material hosted, owned or controlled, or disseminated by an institute. So, the content of an institutional repository is:

Institutionally defined : IR represent an historical and tangible embodiment of the intellectual life and output of an institution;

Scholarly content : This may include pre-prints and other works-in-progress, peer reviewed articles, monographs, conference papers, theses and dissertations, etc.

Cumulative and perpetual : IR aims to preserve and make accessible digital content on a long-term basis; and

Open and interoperable : IR systems must be able to support interoperability in order to provide access via multiple search engines and other discovery tools.

CONTENTS OF AN INSTITUTIONAL REPOSITORY

- Pre-prints of articles or research reports submitted for publication
- The text of articles accepted for publication in journal
- Revised of published work with comments for academic readers
- Conference paper
- Teaching materials
- Students projects
- Doctorial thesis and dissertations
- Databases resulting for research projects
- Committee paper
- Computer software
- Works of art
- Photographs and video recordings

Setting-up an IR requires infrastructural resources, like:-

- Repository server and adequate network bandwidth.
- Human resources – Appropriate manpower for installation, configuration and administration of the repository software and server, and manpower for content management and collection development
- Management commitment and long term funding support
- Development of policies, metadata and cataloguing
- Selection of repository software system
- Advocacy for getting content by encouraging researches and faculty members to participate in IR

- Dissemination and extension of services

One of the SR Ranganathan's 'Five Laws of Library Science' wrote in 1931 "A library is a growing organism". This indicates that the library must be willing to adapt new conditions (changing social and technological conditions as well as changing needs among its clientele), if it is to meet its goal of maximizing accessibility and exposure while minimizing the user's time and effort. Moreover, now information is considered as one of the natural resource. So, developing digital repositories system would be an essential to make information resource more accessible. It would be a collaborative effort, of major stake–holders, who can play an important role in developing IR, such as – Librarian and Library staff, IT personnel, faculty, researchers, students, administration & Finance, etc.

KEY ISSUES RELATED TO IR:

- Proper policies related to types and formats of documents to be considered for IR, along with issues, like user permissions and rights, peer-review and quality assessment of open access material. It is suggested that for perpetual license, the author should be asked to grant the right to the institution to preserve and distribute the research and others work through IR.
- Organization of content : It is a well known fact that finding information on the Internet is only half job done. Researchers and scientists spend more time analyzing information than they do finding it. Therefore, organization of content, cataloguing, metadata and assigning subjects may be properly planned and implemented. Otherwise, we may require human search engine for analyzing information for researchers and scientists.
- Selection of IR software and other related requirements would be clear fully identified.

- Administration and maintenance of IR :- Identify a suitable person as an in-charge who would be responsible for collection development, promotion & dissemination of services

IMPORTANCE OF DEVELOPING INSTITUTIONAL REPOSITORY

The building of an Institutional Repository for any organization is needed in the present scenario of digital world because of the following certain changes:

- Significant increase in the overall volume of research;
- Increasing need of archival and access to unpublished information bearing objects;
- Increasing demand to access knowledge objects from anywhere at any time;

In view of the above changes in the present scenario, developing institutional repositories become very important and essential for the institutions. It will provide a window that gives open access to improve the institution's visibility and status and also support the open-access model of publication. Academic work available on the internet may read more widely than work published in paper format. Depositing academic work in university repository, therefore, increases the profile of an author worldwide, and increases both the dissemination and the impact of the research they undertake. The main advantages of IR are:

For Users

- Expansion of the range of shared knowledge
- Opportunities to simplify and extend dissemination

For the contributor

- Greater citation, digital platform to publish publications, preservation of the publications in digital form, easy to reuse.

For Institutions

- Enabling of IPR to be exploited more effectively at institutional level.
- Flexible ways to develop exiting scholarly communications
- Opportunities for new forms of scholarly communications
- Flexible ways to develop existing scholarly communications

For Researcher Community

- The research community will be able to access the world's research available in different Institutional Repositories
- IR helps for faster communication and reduces the unwanted duplication

INSTITUTIONAL REPOSITORIES IN INDIA

There are numbers of software are available in market for institutional Repository. Some of them are on pay basis and some are free downloaded software for example: DSpace, GNU E-prints, CD-Sware, Fedora, and Greenstone. Among them DSpace, Greenstone, E-print are free software. Some of institutional repositories in India and software used by them are as on Table 1.

ROLE OF IR IN IMPROVING VISIBILITY AND IMPACT OF RESEARCH

Historically, the library's primary research function has been to gather and organize information to provide a meaningful structure for faculty and researchers who synthesize information in building knowledge. Librarians have performed this function well in the past and have been aggressive in responding to the opportunities offered by the newer information technologies. Whereas the lack of access to needed information was the major problem in pre-Internet days, today too much information and

Table 5.1. Institutional Repositories in India

Sr. No.	Institution	URL	Types of Documents	Software Used
1.	INFLIBNET, Infocity, Gandhinagar, Gujrat	*http://dspace.inflibnet.ac.in*	Publications; Conferences; Articles; Theses; Reports; Unpublished learning objects; multimedia; patents (Multidisciplinary)	DSpace
2.	ETD of Indian Institute of Science (IISC), Banglore	*http://eprints.iisc.ernet.in*	Thesis & Dissertations (Multidisciplinary)	E-print
3.	Documentation Research & Training Center (DRTC), Banglore	*https://drtc.isibang.ac.in*	Publications (Research papers, Articles); Reports; Conferences; Theses; Multimedia, etc.	DSpace
4.	Indian Institute of Management, Kozhikode (IIMK)	*http://dspace.iimk.ac.in*	Publications (Research papers, Articles); Conference proceedings; Unpublished Theses (Business & Economics); Reports, etc.	DSpace
5.	Indian Institute of Information Technology, Allahabad	*http://eprints.iiita.ac.in*	Research paper, Article, Reports, etc.	E-print
6.	Indian Institute of Technology, Delhi (IITD)	*http://eprint.iitd.ac.in/dspace*	Post-prints (Research papers, Articles); Theses (Multidisciplinary); Reports, etc.	DSpace
7.	Indian National Science Academy (INSA), Banglore	*http://61.16.154.195/dspace*	Conference Papers, Articles, Reports, etc.	DSpace
8.	Indian Statistical Institute, Banglore	*http://library.isibang.ac.in:8080/dspace*	Research papers, Articles, Reports, etc.	DSpace

9.	National Chemical Laboratory (NCL), Pune	*http://dspace.ncl.res.in*	Theses; Patents; Research papers; Articles; Reports, etc.	DSpace
10.	Vidyanidhi Digital Library at University of Mysore	*http://www.vidyanidhi.org.in*	Theses and Dissertations	DSpace
11.	National Institute of Technology Rourkela	*http://dspace.nitrkl.ac.in/dspace/*	Publications (Research Papers); Preprints; Conference Proceedings; Patents; Thesis; Multimedia, etc.	DSpace
12.	National Informatics Centre (NIC), New Delhi	*http://www.nic.in/publication*	Publications (Reports, Proceedings, etc.)	EPrints
13.	National Aerospace Laboratories	*http://nal-ir.nal.res.in/*	Publications; Conference proceedings; Theses; Unpublished Learning Objects; Multimedia; Patents, etc.	GNU-EPrints
14.	Indian Institute of Technology, Bombay	*http://dspace.library.iitb.ac.in/jspui/*	Theses & Dissertation book chapters, conference proceedings, technical reports, journal pre-prints & post-prints, working papers, Patents and annual reports etc.	Greenstone
15.	National Centre for Catalysis, Chennai	*http://www.eprints.iitm.ac.in/*	Publications; Conference proceedings; Theses, etc.	GNU-EPrints
16.	National Institute of Oceanography (NIO), Panaji, Goa	*http://drs.nio.org/drs/*	journal articles, conference proceeding articles, Technical reports, thesis, dissertations, etc.	DSpace

the need for time and tools of efficiently "fish" for the needed scholarly material are of prime concern to scholars. The over abundance of materials produced has seriously clogged the scholarly communications system. By linking different types of information sources and providing easy-to-use tools to search across multiple databases, librarians have supported researchers' ability to handle the overabundance of information available, as interdisciplinary studies continue to expand and as faculty build global perspectives into exiting courses, this linking function of academic libraries will become even more important to researchers. Now, libraries are playing the central role in supporting research.

For librarians, the challenge of the past has been linking information among various subject areas. The challenge of the future will be to incorporate digitized information in a way that "preserves the linkages to the existing knowledge base, encourages and stimulates the productive use of new technologies, and provides coordinated gateway access to the universe of knowledge in a manner convenient and invisible to the end user." The essence of IR is to make research and development publications to be freely available on the internet. This initiative will increase the visibility of the research outcomes. Institutional initiatives to promote open access to the research work carried out by them, has been made possible through establishing Institutional Repositories. These are "digital archives of intellectual products created by the faculty, staff and students of an institution or group of institutions accessible to end users both within and without the institution. ICT has changed the whole library and information landscape in the world. However, in the developing countries in general and India in particular, the situation is not so encouraging except some national institutions and well reputed universities have started to work in developing digital repositories. But, the trend towards in the direction shows that very soon a large number of the academic institutions will join their hands in the movement and get their visibility of academic importance published and makes the research output available to the worldwide.

ROLE OF LIBRARIES

The library plays a crucial role in an information society-connecting, integrating, and managing informational resources. The value of the library for the academic community is not less than in pre-Internet days, but far greater in the present era. Librarians have always been engaged in managing and developing their collection, LIS professionals are always in font of new technology and they accept it and trying to develop their library services. Librarians have long experience for collection building and maintain the information. Institutional Repository and open access will be the next challenge for Library and LIS professionals. As a result libraries have to play vital role in building Institutional Repositories. Libraries are able to provide direct access to scholarly publication via IR rather than any other. The Institutional Repositories are successful because of its new information and current information. It's related with producer of being responsible for adding an item to a repository and creating the associated metadata and the libraries the lead role in development of the institutional repositories and their normalization with collection management. Institutional Repositories needs satisfactory and trained staffing support having knowledge of Institutional repository and to overcome this problem library would have to train their staff member or would have to requite librarians who have good knowledge about IR and who can handle well digital collection management.

The active involvement and support of the academic library staff and resources will be a key to students acquiring lifelong learning abilities and faculty achieving greater research productivity. In partnership with academic administrators and classroom faculty, librarians can enhance instruction, research, and service while supporting the eventual transformation of higher education. After all these things the only single work is remained that the Institute's head have to invest the money of it needs funding by using the LIS staff can build a good IR and deliver their Information Facilities to development their institute.

CONCLUSION

Institutional Repository (IR) has emerged as a new model for Scholarly Publishing and Communication. IR is becoming popular in institutions of higher education as it has potential to bring significant benefits to institutions (e.g. imposed visibility, status and public value, and effective knowledge management) and also individual researchers (e.g. impact of research). In India, however, it still depends on the more traditional information sources. Though a lot of good work are being carried out by the institutes but never reaches to the user community, simply has not been published. The classified reports containing valuable data or information are lost forever due to the security reasons. But, it is well known fact that the development of nations now depends upon their ability to compete in the knowledge society.

It is only possible when India's indigenous achievements in the field of Science and Technology are available in electronic format and disseminate to researchers & information professionals in both India and the wider scientific world. An effort needs to be done collectively to preserve and share our invaluable knowledge globally and over come a serious barrier of digital divide. According to R.N. Mashelkar, if India plays its card right it can become by 2020 the world's number one knowledge production centre. So, IRs can play an important role to accelerate the use of electronic information resources in Indian libraries and research centres to become the centre of excellence for knowledge workers, innovators of the future, and hub of global R & D activities. University libraries and the librarians have to play a major role in developing successful digital repositories for their institutions and these institutional repositories can build the great visibility and impact of the institutions and their academic community and finally, establish the impact of our country on a global map.

REFERENCES

Bhogle, Srinivas. (2005). Turning pages; reflections in Info-times. Bangalore.

Centre for Science & Environment (2005). Basics of Digital Library (course material).

Crow, Raym. (2002). The case for Institutional repositories: A SPARC position paper.

Rajashekar, T. B. (2004). Institutional repositories. U & I (January issue)

Rajashekar, T.B. (2004). Institutional repositories: Improving preservation, organization and dissemination of institutional research (tutorial). ICDL 2004, TERI: (New Delhi).

Barton, M. R., & Waters, M. M. (2004). Creating an Institutional Repository: LEADIRS Workbook.

Drake, M. A. (2004). Institutional Repositories: Hidden Treasures. *Information Today, 12*(5), New York.

Kanchan, K. (2009). Institutional Repository projects in India. *CALIBER 2009* (pp. 128-132). Pondicherry: INFLIBNET Centre Ahmedabad.

6

Institutional Repository : A Performance Indicator

K. Chinnasamy

INTRODUCTION

The Open Access Initiative, Author self-archiving and Web servers are older version of Institutional Repositories. IR's are digital collections of that workforce intellectual capital wherein they preserve and provide access to an institutional community for scholarly communication. An institutional repository is a means to collect the intellectual digital output of an organization. The universities, Colleges, or any other organization store treasures of intellectual capital and they have been hidden in the form of archives at basement floor. The Open Access pave a way for Institutional Repository. Generally these intellectual products are unavailable to researchers, public or the workforce of the organization.

The open access and open archives movement for scholarly communication removes barriers to access and increase the development of IR in higher education institutes. The basic purpose behind this is to collect and preserve the intellectual capital of an organization for further developments and act as performance indicator for their intellectual capital.

IR is marketing tools for scholarly communicating and capabilities of intellectual of the workforce of any organization. The Universities or colleges IR consist of working papers, pre-prints, journal articles, teaching and learning resources, question papers and other document regarding the recognition and its related documents of corresponding apex body and any funded research projects are made available particularly to its users and to public in general.

WHAT IS AN INSTITUTIONAL REPOSITORY?

An IR is a service that an organization offers to its workforce for the management and dissemination of intellectual output created by its own workforce. The main purpose is to collect- organize- conserve-preserve-indexes- access to their intellectual capital All it needs digital and standard metadata software. It is also acts as a benchmark of an institution for its existences. The IR may contain research articles, funded or not funded research reports, conference proceedings, teaching and learning resources, theses and or dissertations, institutional records, etc are basic collections here.

The Institutional Repository is generally a "Digital archives of intellectual products created by the faculty, staff and students of an institution accessible to its users and general public."

OPEN SOURCE

Open source doesn't just mean access to the source code. The distribution terms of open source software must comply with the following criteria.

Free Redistribution : The license shall not restrict any part from selling or giving away the software as a component of an aggregate software distribution containing programs from several different sources. The license shall not require a royalty or other fee for such sale.

Source Code : The program must include source code, and must allow distribution in source code as well as compiled form. Where some form of a product is not distributed with source code, there must be a well-publicized means of obtaining the source code for no more than a reasonable reproduction cost preferably, downloading via the Internet without charge. The source code must be the preferred form in which a programmer would modify the program. Deliberately obfuscated source code is not allowed. Intermediate forms such as the output of a preprocessor or translator are not allowed.

Derived Works : The license must allow modifications and derived works, and must allow them to be distributed under the same terms as the license of the original software.

Integrity of the Author's Source Code : The license may restrict source-code from being distributed in modified form only if the license allows the distribution of "patch files" with the source code for the purpose of modifying the program at build time. The license must explicitly permit distribution of software built from modified source code. The license may require derived works to carry a different name or version number from the original software.

- The license must not discriminate against any person or group of persons.
- The license must not restrict anyone from making use of the program in a specific field of endeavor. For example, it may not restrict the program from being used in a business, or from being used for genetic research.
- The rights attached to the program must apply to all to whom the program is redistributed without the need for execution of an additional license by

those parties.

- The rights attached to the program must not depend on the program's being part of a particular software distribution. If the program is extracted from that distribution and used or distributed within the terms of the program's license, all parties to whom the program is redistributed should have the same rights as those that are granted in conjunction with the original software distribution.
- The license must not place restrictions on other software that is distributed along with the licensed software. For example, the license must not insist that all other programs distributed on the same medium must be open- source software.
- License Must Be Technology- Neutral. No provision of the license may be predicated on any individual technology or style of interface.

OPEN SOURCE SYSTEM

Open source system may be classified under the following heads:

- Open Source Library Software: Library Manager, Library Management System, GPL Library
- Loan Management System, Greenstone3, Librarian DB, NewGenLib. Content Management Software: Drupal, Joomla
- Institutional Repository Software: DSpace, Eprint
- Other OSS Resource: Open Source System for Libraries (OSS4LIB), National Research Centre for free/ Open Source Software (NRCFOSS), Open Source Software Repository (Sourceforge), UNESCO Free & Open Software Portal (Link).

DIGITAL REPOSITORY SOFTWARE

"Digital Repository Software" is primarily used in academic libraries who are involved in building institutional repositories of their institution's intellectual scholarship and other born digital works.

DSpace

Originally developed at MIT, *DSpace* is an open source software used for building digital repositories. DSpace preserves and provides access to various types of digital content including text, images, moving images, mpegs, and data sets.

Greenstone

Greenstone is an open source option for building and providing access to digital library collections. Greenstone is produced by the New Zealand Digital Library Project at the University of Waikato.

Fedora Commons Repository Software

Originally developed at Cornell University, *Fedora Commons* is another open source software available for building digital repositories.

EPrints

This is a *free and open-source software* package for building *open access* repositories that are compliant with the *Open Archives Initiative Protocol for Metadata Harvesting* (OAI-PMH). It shares many of the features commonly seen in *document management systems*, but is primarily used for *institutional repositories* and *scientific journals.[1]* EPrints has been developed at the *University of Southampton School of Electronics and Computer Science* and released under a *GPL* license.

WHY INSTITUTIONAL REPOSITORIES?

A repository enables faculty, researchers, and administrators who want to archive research, historic, and creative materials. The open access and open archives movement, the need fcr changes in scholarly communication to remove barriers to access, and the increasing awareness that universities and research institutions are losing valuable digital and print materials are the main reasons for the establishment of institutional repositories. Using open archive models, established metadata standards, and digital rights management; new and important information sources are increasingly available. While the main purpose of institutional repositories are to bring together and preserve the intellectual output of a laboratory, department, university, or other entity. The incentives and commitments to change the process of scholarly communication have also begun and serving as strong motivators. Computers have been ubiquitous on campuses since late 1980s and students and faculty are comfortable with the power of online communication.

Faculty teachers and researchers want to archive their own materials and have them available on personal or institutional Web sites, these articles, along with the development of the Internet and more powerful search engines, have enabled people to think in practical terms about the establishment of central facilities for storing, archiving, preserving, and making scholarly and artistic materials available. Repositories may be limited to one field, one department, one institution, or a consortium of several institutions. Collaboration through a consortium reduces costs for each member through resource sharing while expanding access to digital materials.

Scholarly societies may establish discipline-based repositories to preserve the history and literature of a particular subject area. However, these societies have a serious dilemma. They publish journals to disseminate research about their fields. If the societies establish open access repositories, they could experience reduced or zero publishing profits, which might in turn affect their ability to pay overhead expenses and to provide enhanced member services. The loss of revenue could place these societies in the position of having to ask members to pay more of the cost of member services.

The increasing demand for scholarly information, especially in science, will probably increase the pressure on scholarly societies and universities. Digital publishing, global networking, more research, and increased communication among communities of scholars are driving the demand for broader access. The idea of the invisible college nurtured by meetings and preprints of journal articles has been replaced by global, discipline- or project-based online communities. Governments and its agencies may use repositories in the same ways as universities are doing. Some agencies will find repositories useful for storage and access to technical reports, white papers, hearings, and other documents.

BENEFITS OF INSTITUTIONAL REPOSITORIES

IR by collecting, organising, conserving, preserving, indexing and providing access to its intellectual capital acts as worthy parameter for research or academic quality. This pushes into gauge its own productivity and stake claim for its accreditation. The benefits are classified as follows;

For the Individual

Provides and acts as a platform for their central archives activity of their scholarly work and provides wider accessibility. It is a medium for faster dissemination and increase the readership of their work. Further, it helps to recognise individuals and their work in particular and the institution in general.

For the Institution

It helps to preserves the heritage of the institution and increases visibility of the institution and draws more readerships. It acts as a quality benchmark to obtain funds and impact factor and would be able to attract potential workforce, stakeholders, etc.

For Society

Provide wide access to the unpublished and/or grey literatures to the various stakeholders and serves strong motivators for scholarly communication. Preserving the intellectual capital for the long term and present it to the world.

PROBLEMS ASSOCIATED WITH IR

- Lack of proper policy - A crucial part is deciding what to collect, what to store, what to preserve and what to discard is to be addressed.
- Insufficient funds for required IT Infrastructure for refreshing and migration and trained manpower.
- Protocols for interoperability and software are delicate.
- As the IR is bookshelves of digital content none of the storage media can be guaranteed to last long.
- Time consuming and lengthy deposition procedure for its management leads to the authors and publishers annoyed.
- Sustainability is the major issue
- Lack of awareness and copyright infringement is also an issue to overcome.

MEASURES FOR SUCCESSFUL IR

Following measures are necessary in building successful Institutional Repositories viz., eight "C" words:

1. Comprehension : workforce must share and understand the scope and purpose of the repository

2. Collaboration : collaboration involves thinking and working together to contribute scholarly communication and to solve the common problems

3. Context : each employee has a unique mind set and education, work culture and experience helps them to integrate for contribution

4. Change : mould employee to feel as an institutional asset for intellectual capital deposition

5. Caring : motivate them to share their contribution for dissemination and growth

6. Commitment : for continuous growth and funding in time without end

7. Creativity : constellation of an imaginary object and to visualize them

8. Competence : know-how of IR elements and its functions.

CONCLUSION

IR has brought an illustrative changes and wider openings in the field of scholarly publication. Development of IR has received a little leverage from the workforce and publishers for change and commitment. The IR acts as seamless tool to capture, store, preserve and to access intellectual capital of scholars. Further, it simplifies the process of global access to local information. There is no doubt that the open access features of IR could contribute significantly to economic growth by broadening the area of market for scholarly publications.

REFERENCES

Crow, Raym. (2002). The case for institutional repositories: A SPARC Position Paper Scholarly Publishing and Academic Resources Coalition.

Johnson, Richard. (2002). Institutional repositories: Partnering with faculty to enhance scholarly communication. D-Lib Magazine.

Moorthy, A. L. (2010). Institutional repositories and their benefits for an organization.

Arms, Williams. Y. (2005). Digital libraries. New Delhi; Ane Books.

Kumar, P. S. G. (2004). Information technology: Applications. Delhi; B R Publishing Corp.

Website

Association of Research Libraries. Retrieved from http://*www.arl.org/* SPARC/IR/ir.html.

7

Building a Sustainable Institutional Repository : Some Guidelines

N B Dahibhate
Sujata Hargude

INTRODUCTION

Institutional Repositories (IRs) is a new initiative in managing digital objects of intellectual contributions for effective utilization in academic and research organization. IR development is a challenge and opportunity for information professionals, and includes compilation of intellectual and research output of an organization. An IR is a means to ensure that the published work of scholars is available to the academic community even after increases in subscription fees or budget cuts within libraries (Bhardwaj, 2014 & Boufarss 2011). IRs provide scholars with a common platform to contribute scholarly material to promote cross-campus interdisciplinary research. An institutional repository is an online archive for collecting, preserving, and disseminating digital intellectual output of an institution, particularly a research institution.

An institutional repository can be viewed as "a set of services that a university offers to members of its community for the management and dissemination of digital materials created by the institution and its community members" (Lynch 2003). IR includes information materials such as monographs, pre-prints of academic journal articles and post-prints after obtaining permission from publisher of peer reviewed articles, as well as electronic theses and dissertations (ETDs) etc. An institutional repository might also include other digital assets generated by academics, such as datasets, administrative documents, course notes, learning objects, or conference proceedings. Deposit of material in an institutional repository is sometimes mandated by that institution. (*https://en.wikipedia.org/wiki/Institutional_repository*).

The main objectives for developing an institutional repository is to provide open access to institutional research output by self-archiving to create global visibility for an institution's scholarly research, and to store and preserve other institutional digital assets, including unpublished or otherwise "grey" literature such as theses, working papers or technical reports etc. There are few open-source software packages available for developing IR like DSpace, EPrints, Fedora Commons, Greenstone etc.

WHAT IS IR?

The meaning of institutional repository is "a facility for storing and maintaining digital information in accessible form. It is also called as "Digital Archive" also. Repositories use different technologies for storage and distribution of digital contents. Wiki has represented IR as "an Institutional Repository is an online locus for collecting, preserving, and disseminating — in digital form — the intellectual output of an institution, particularly a research institution". (en.wikipedia.org/wiki/Institutional

Repositories).

Narayana (2009) defined "Digital archives of intellectual products created by faculty, staff and students of an institution or group of institutions accessible to end users both within and outside the institution". IR is also called as a web based database (repository) of scholarly material. IR collects stores and disseminates digital resources and efforts made for long term preservation of organizational or institutional intellectual property in digital form. The main aim behind development of IR is to organize the literature published as an intellectual and scholarly output of grey literature of an institute in full text from and provide open access by self archiving at institute.

REASON FOR DEVELOPING IR

IR is now essential for the academic and research institutes to highlight treasure of the institute have hidden grey literature, which never appeared in the public domain. Academic institutes, universities, museums, government's academic institutes, and other organizations houses treasure of information that have been hidden as archives. This treasure encompasses scientific, technological, cultural, artistic, and historical data generally unavailable to searchers and to the public easily. Institutional repositories are now being created to manage, preserve, and maintain the digital assets, intellectual output, and histories of institutions at one place in IR. Librarians are taking leadership roles in planning and building repositories, and manage roles as experts in collecting, describing, preserving, and providing stewardship for documents and digital information. The reason behind the IR is to collect, analyse, synthesise, organise, the intellectual collection of the institute at one place. This helps users in consulting grey literature.

The main purpose behind developing institutional repositories is to bring together and preserve the intellectual output of a laboratory, department, university, or other educational and research entity. The incentives and commitments to change the process of scholarly communication have also begun serving as strong motivators. Students and faculty are comfortable with the power of online communication. Faculty teachers and researchers want to archive their own materials and have them available on personal or institutional websites. These articles, along with development of the internet and more powerful search engines, have enabled people to think in practical terms about the establishment of central facilities for storing, archiving, preserving, and making scholarly and artistic materials available. Repositories may be limited to one field, one department, one institution, or a consortium of several institutions. Collaboration through consortium reduces costs for each member through resource sharing while expanding access to digital materials. (Drake 2004)

There are many reasons to implement an IR in an institute and few common ones are :

- To increase the visibility and citation impact of institution's scholarship
- To provide unified access to institution's scholarship.
- Support to open access to institution's scholarship
- To create mechanism for sharing information with other institutes
- Avoid duplication efforts
- Provide access to grey and intellectual literature of institute

Pals (2004) stated that universities and research libraries around the world use institutional repository in the following ways:

- Scholarly communication, storing learning materials and courseware's

- Electronic publishing and preserving digital materials for the long term
- Adding to the university's prestige by showcasing its academic research
- Knowledge management and research assessment
- Encouraging open access to scholarly research.
- Each university has a unique culture and assets that require a customized approach.

OBJECTIVES OF IR

Development of high quality scholarly publications from the institutes and developing awareness among the users is the main objective. An IR is multifunctional and can serve a range of educational purposes and the objectives are:

- Provision to the visibility of scholarly publication at local and global level
- Tool for archiving and sharing the resources from the institutional output
- Resource for bringing out the grey literature of organization at one place
- Enhance the reputation of the library and organization
- Support the open access, and bring in to the light the scholarly communication.
- Preservation of all the institutional documents in digital form at central place and making available to others
- Develop open access and self archiving mechanism
- Initiation of marketing efforts

PURPOSE BEHIND ESTABLISHING IR

The main purpose of IR is to capture the publications of the institution in digital form over the web. The preservation of intellectual content for the long run is another purpose.

- Create global visibility and wider access to institute's scholarly publications and research work
- Availability of institute's work at one place and can be accessible to every one
- To provide open access to intellectual literature
- Getting citations to the papers

The purpose is also to provide access to institutional literature to everyone and also share the information. For development of IR the main functions involved are document submission (Verification, Authenticity, uploading etc), Archiving (date, identifier, indexing), Dissemination (Search, browse) administration (maintenance) and user registration and directory maintenance etc. Digital archives of intellectual products created by the faculty, staff and students of an institution or group of institutions accessible to end users both within and outside the institution is the main aim behind IR.

BENEFITS OF INSTITUTIONAL REPOSITORY

Benefits of IR are to individual and institute both. Swan (2009) has lists out few benefits of repositories in institutions:

- Opening up to an outputs of the institution, to a worldwide audience;
- Maximizing the visibility and impact of institutes outputs;
- Collect and curate digital output;
- Managing and measuring research and teaching activities;
- Supporting to a workspace for work-in-progress, and for collaborative or large-scale projects;
- Enabling and encouraging interdisciplinary approaches to research;
- Facilitating the development and sharing of digital

teaching materials and aids

- Supporting student endeavors, providing access to theses and dissertations and a location for the development of e-portfolios or portals.

Apart from these few benefits gained from IR are:

- One stop source of institutional intellectual output. (otherwise it may be unnoticed, scattered and grey)
- Exposure to the available and current activities of the institution, and helps in interdisciplinary research or avoiding the duplication in research.
- There is a possibility of achieving universal access to material, otherwise the data is limited to the subscribers of the journals.
- Easy information discovery is possible as the search engines like Google, Google Scholar, OCLC, opens the contents to users
- Long term preservation of scholarly collection
- IR try to collect content of various types of material published through the institution (more than journal articles)
- It is a prestige to the institution
- It supports to teaching and learning
- Rich resource sharing among scholars
- All the time access 24/7

Repositories provide services to faculty, researchers, and administrators who want to archive research, historic, and creative materials. The open access and open archives movement, the need for changes in scholarly communication to remove barriers to access, and the increasing awareness that universities and research institutions are losing valuable digital and print materials have begun driving the establishment of institutional repositories. Using open archive models, established metadata standards, and digital rights management, important new information sources are seeing the light of day and becoming more generally available. (Drake 2004). Jain et al (http://www.library.up.ac.za/digi/docs/jain_paper.pdf), Pickton and Barwick (2006) also narrated the benefits of IR to the information society viz.

- Increasing the visibility of information and also a prestige to an academic institute.
- Create and share scholarly literature as well as development of mutual exchange of information platform.
- Qualitative IR may be a tool for marketing activities and generating funds.
- Collection and preservation of all grey literature of an organisation at one place.
- Support to virtual learning and teaching process of an organization
- Analyses the research trends of the organisation
- Compilation of research and building network among organisations
- Access to IR from different learning platforms
- Enhance the quality of university information system
- Promoting use of e-publications and digital contents
- Dissemination of information from IR to scientific community
- Benefits to different communities like institution, researchers, learners, students, academicians, information society etc.

SETTING AN IR

Since technologies and software's are available abundantly in the information environment, development of IR is comparatively inexpensive and easy but its sustenance is not easy. The process of building IR mainly includes selection of software, hardware, personals, intellectual content, development of metadata, management support, finance, IPR issues etc. The basic requirements for establishing IR are:

Hardware : High end dedicated servers with high storage capacity for holding and storing / preserving data. Hardware configuration generally required is, computer workstation with one data server of capacity 2.8-3.5 GHz (Quad core) RAM = 8 to 16 GB, HDD = 1TB to 2 TB or even higher. Other equipments like scanners, digital and movie cameras, UPS, printers, CD drives or tape drives etc. with operating system Linux (Red Hat) RHEL 4/5. But availability of free open software's for development of IR, helped institutes to develop IR. Among many any of the following is preferred and commonly used for creation of IR.

Software selection : Though many open source software's are available, but there is a need to evaluate them for the use and select appropriate one for development of IR. From the survey it is observed that Eprint, Dspace, Fedora are few but Dspace is used more. E-prints (University of Southampton, UK, http://software.eprints.org), D-space (MIT + HP USA, http://www.dspace.org), Fedora (Cornell University and Virginia university USA, www.fedora.info), i-tor (Netherland Institute fro scientific information services, www.i-tor.org), Green Stone (new Zealand digital library project Uni. of Waikato, www.greenstone.org) ,CD Sware (CERN document server software, Geneva Switzerland, http://cdsware.cern.ch.) are available. Out of these Eprints, fedora, Greenstone, D-space are very popularly used. Apart from these IR softwares, few open source softwares are also required like : Scanning and OCR software, Adobe acrobat PDF converter and reader, CD read/write software, PageMaker, paint brush, Windows-NT networking software, SQL server software, Database management software. Web designing software like JAVA, Front page, XML etc. , RDBMS supporting the variety of digital database like ORACLE, My SQL etc. , Full text search engines to index and provide access.

Staff for managing IR : Trained staff for development, management and maintenance of IR and capable of handling problems. Good administrator to develop policies to sustain IR for longer run. ICT trained manpower is more beneficial. A group of staff involved in developing IR is librarian or library staff, administrative staff, ICT staff etc.

Contents : IR content covers intellectual assets of institute, compiled for users and can retrieve information when ever needed by users. Generally content covers e-books, e-Journal articles, chapters from books, newspaper articles, conference papers (preprint from) in digital form, technical reports, proceeding's, uunpublished materials like historical record, manuscripts, rare collection, doctoral theses and dissertations, teaching material, research notes / data / information, photos, audio data, grey literature, patents, archival documents, posters, event celebrations, speeches of eminent personalities, learning and teaching objects, class notes, presentations, library and laboratory guides, subject guides, question papers, manuals, internal circulated documents, annual reports, working papers, university publications, notices, newsletters, circulars and syllabus etc. In brief all scientific, technical, educational, research, artistic, teaching, output of institution is the content of IR to build document management system. All public domain literature can be covered in IR which is free from IPR. Rajashekar (2010) indicated that the content is in digital form might be born or digitized and in different file formats developed by members of the institutions. The nature of access to these content is either free or registration based or membership based to anyone.

Contributors to IR : Authors, teachers, learners, researchers, reviewers, institute as publishing agency etc.

Policies : Different policies need to be formulated like selection of software and hardware, contents, management, addition and retention policies, access policies and information dissemination policy. These are needed for sustaining even in adverse condition.

- Respect to IPR issues, additional funds to get components.
- Phase wise initiation of IR consist of identification of contents, document evaluation for inclusion, institutional information, authorization of staff for maintaining IR, legality issue consideration, fixing metadata elements (descriptive or structural), uploading data and quality control of IR.
- Fixing items and kind of items inclusion with IPR (published and non published), authorization for inclusion in IR form authors, access facilities (in-house or external).
- The approximate initial cost required for the initiation of this activity varies from institute to institute but minimum Rs 3-4 Lack at initial level is required to develop the IT platform required for the IR. The process of development also includes: material selection and submission, development of metadata (Fix the elements), access control, information discovery support (Index building), distribution of the information and preservation.

SKILLS REQUIRED FOR DEVELOPING IR

There is a need to acquire skills for developing, maintaining, managing and sustaining IR. Few skills required are:

1. Management skills

- Manage IR as per the user needs
- Prepare costing for building repository
- Manage day today working of IR

- Develop policies for sustainable IR
- Fix the type of deposit (global or at the nodal point)
- Handle complaints, and relationship

2. Software skills

- Software awareness is more important while developing the IR.
- The required software's like Unix, Linux, MySQL, SGML, XML, JAVA, PERL etc. are preferred for IR
- Trained in any one of software Eprints, Dspace or Fedora etc.

3. Metadata

For making the digital objects available at global level, it is necessary to adapt relevant metadata standards Dublin core, MARC, OAI PMH which helps in developing metadata and monitor metadata quality for IR.

4. Storage and Preservation

It is a key function of the IR and work with IT services for the use of network storage and backup of the data. It is necessary to make provision for the long term storage and identify best practices and preserve the documents. Develop a policy for different materials for its display and preservation and also fix the file format (pdf) for storage of data.

5. Content Development

The documents captured must be authenticated by relevant IPR issues and suitable guide lines to be prepared to ensure good practices. For building contents of IR:

- Develop a content policy
- Categorize the material for deposit
- Management of submission and withdrawal of documents from the repository
- Increase the quality and quantity of material in the

repository

- Identify suitable documents from the personal and departmental web pages
- Encourage the authors for the deposition of publication

6. Liaison

Liaison within the organization and outside the organization is required for utility of IR to information community. For this purpose administrator has to perform following tasks:

- Liaise with several departments and interested groups
- Identify high level and long term institutional strategies, needs, which can be met through the repository
- Frame practical policies and procedures so that repository becomes embedded in the research process of the institution
- Create the awareness of benefits of IR among the users
- Channelize the process for the publishing material and it could be to routed through a publication committee, this may help in monitoring the publications and also inclusion in the IR later.
- Liaise with IT staff and maintain HW and SW
- Initiate the contacts with individual scientist / research groups to identify their needs.
- Promote the repository outside the institution and propagate the institutional work. The repository must be registered with the Directory of Open Access Repository (Open DOAR), Open Access Initiatives (OAI).

CHALLENGES IN MAINTAINING IR

Pickton and Barwick (2006) has discussed challenges faced by librarians in developing IR. Among the different challenges cost is the major factor in spite of the availability of free open source software's available. The staff cost, equipments, training, creation of metadata, etc. involve cost. Successful IR need contents creation and regular updates from the contributors to deposit the work in the repository for its long run. Management support is required to develop, maintain and update IR by providing facilities to the developer and preparing different policies for the sustenance.

The most important challenge is to follow IPR issues properly. The administrator need to be motivated by incentives. Quality maintenance and standard data entry in IR and providing services to users is an intellectual task and librarians have to face the challenges. Barton et al (2005) has pointed out many problems and hurdles faced while implementation and building a repository includes: Proper development of policies and its sustainability, managing intellectual property rights for common use and awareness, management or institutional support as well as users support, digital preservation and identifying key stakeholders, it also needs personalized efforts of library staff to collect, scan and preserve and make it available on demand. This needs extra skills for maintaining IR.

POLICIES FOR IR

To develop sustainable IR there is need to prepare different policies useful for the IR initiation, development and maintenance. Each institute has to develop repository policy, which coverers the commitments by institute, administrator, manager and authors or contributors. While establishing repositories there are a variety of decisions librarians or administrator has to take. Policies, systems architecture, and other elements depend on institutional context and the scope and purposes of the repository. Some of the key issues to consider when developing repositories are: institutional culture, scope of the repository, content of IR, access levels, legal aspects, standards, sustainability and funding. The main points to be considered while drafting policy may be:

- Contributors to IR (authors, contributors)
- Incentives to contributors to deposit document in the repository
- Quality control
- IR management and maintenance issues
- contents inclusion and preservation period, kind of documents to be added
- Protection of IPR and copyright
- uploading documents in IR and period of updating IR

The different policies need to be developed due to following reasons:

- To build the culture of trust and cooperative environment amongst the staff and management.
- Decide the scope of IR and communicate with management and staff in advance and decisions may be taken to develop and include contents which could centrally shared and also shared globally. Access policies differ institution to institution. Many institutions prefer to provide access to IR to selected users (password protected contents) or access to material on request only. Many institutions appoint a committee for content creation, deposition, evaluation and circulation.
- It is necessary to ensure all legal requirements are met while developing and inclusion of contents in IR. The main requirements includes appropriate software and legal contents. Many universities have developed comprehensive intellectual property

policies for setting IR, including responsibilities of faculty and administration. Academic institutions usually opt for open access but may have to restrict access for some research activities.

- IR cannot be sustained without long-term infusions of funds. A repository cannot run by itself. It needs constant attention, maintenance and funding. Policies concerning deposit, accessibility, and other anticipated contingencies help in problem-solving process. Everyone, involved in a repository needs to understand importance of project and act for their role effectively.

a) Policy for pre-published contents

i. Written permission of copyright owner (author, publisher).

ii. Copyright expired contents.

iii. Abstract and summaries.

iv. Only metadata or metadata with link of original source.

b) Policy for new contents

i. New generated contents with copyright declaration in prescribed format as per decided by the university with peer review and originality verification of plagiarism.

ii. A new publication published anywhere in any journal or source but keep a pre-print copy in IR mandatorily.

c) Policy for Dual publishing contents

Contents may publish in any journal or other form and IR by special permission or copyright agreement or a clause of copyright agreement allowing to do so. At one side it may be available as per copyright owner's policy and at another side it may available and accessible in institutional premises from IR.

d) Policy for Open Access contents (freely, publicly, promptly available)

i. Compulsion for submission of research output from the university or institute.

ii. Method for depositing content.

iii. Commercial journals sometimes opt for bold publishing and its cost may be varied from publisher to publisher for passing out the copyright.

iv. Open access content which are peer reviewed only.

e) Policy for access control / authorization of the users.

Authorization of the users or access to the contents should be maintained keeping respect of the copyright of each document in IR.

f) Policy for acquisition of contents

i. Acquisition of contents should be as per the policies defined and adopted by the university and input of the acquired content to the IR should be either centralized or under the observation of deputed moderator.

ii. Some publishers permit to include published document in IR after elapsing 6 – 12 months or more.

SUSTAINABILITY AND FUNDING

Maintenance and sustainability are key issues that involve the long-term commitment of IR management. A repository cannot run by itself. It needs constant attention. Maintenance of content, software, and accessibility can change. IT staff and librarians need to know the consequences of changes in hardware, software, and standards and be able to adjust accordingly. Having clear policies concerning deposit, accessibility, and other anticipated contingencies may ease the problem-solving process. Repositories cannot be sustained without long-term infusions of funds. Everyone involved in a repository needs to understand that the project has become part of their everyday lives and requires attention and funding in perpetuity. Too often managers in corporations seem unable to look beyond the quarter's bottom line and shy away from long term commitments. Their reluctance to commit funds is an uncertain economy. Many managers in academe emulate their corporate colleagues through their reluctance to raise and dedicate enough money to ensure that the repository is funded at an appropriate level forever.

Establishing functional IR can help in growing research, scholarly communication, academic collaboration, part in learning and teaching etc. To achieve the goals of IR and quality issues, developer of IR has to consider different elements from design, selection of HW and SW, installation, training, operation, contents uploading, submission, preservation, retention, IPR, data retrieval and reuse of data in the form of services etc. are to be managed well . Major three elements are crucial in IR i.e. authors or creators of intellectual component in different form, administrator and manager of IR and management supporting for financial aspects.

ROLE OF LIBRARIANS IN DEVELOPING IR

Jain et al (2009) are of the opinion that activity and responsibilities relating to IRs are assumed by different people in various institutions. But this activity could be undertaken collaboratively by officers within the library in partnership with research and development, and information technology sections.. Nixon (2002) also rightly observed that "Reference librarians are library's eyes and ears. They understand user's needs and perceptions. They are the library's primary liaison with faculty in their subject areas and its most visible representatives. For an IR to succeed, it is essential that they may be involved in its planning, implementation, and operation". Librarians have to play critical roles in both establishing and maintaining an IR. Librarian is the key person in managing IR as he is the expert person who can index and develop metadata as compared to others. Librarian if appointed as caretaker and administrator for IR then he has to perform different role at a time.

- Formulation of different policies useful for developing, managing and sustaining IR
- Promotion of open access concepts to faculty and try to change the mind for sharing in IR
- Development for encouragement for self archiving
- Metadata development
- Creating community and collection of institute of subject to develop IR and subject IR
- Developing communication among different communities of institute
- Assisting in supporting advantages of IR to contributors by providing services using IR content, getting more citations, web visibility to data etc
- Follow the legality concepts (IPR) while including data in IR
- Selection of proper HW, SW and train manpower for effective management of IR
- Create personal space for contributors, authors and supports to load personal profile, publication list, bio data, research data etc. over IR
- Creation of an interoperable, collaborative and sustainable IR.
- Evaluation of IR frequently to assess its use and benefits to information society.

The role of the librarian is very critical in developing and maintaining IR like:

Advocacy : Librarians need to know all about the IR, its principles, benefits and operational processes in order to promote it and act as 'IR evangelists'

Building content : Librarians can employ advocacy and marketing strategies to promote engagement with faculty members and help to generate content. They assist by proactively searching for content independently.

Collection administrators and metadata specialists : Librarians have potential roles as collection administrators and metadata specialists. For effective implementation of IR, libraries need to recruit IT staff or train librarians with digital collection management and provide a mediated deposit service for reluctant 'self-archives'.

Training : Librarians can train staff and students to use the IR and help them to prepare their digital products.

INDIAN EFFORTS

In India, efforts are made towards direction of developing IR and many universities, research organizations like CSIR, IIM, IIT institutes are developing IRs. Few prominent IR developed and working are: IIT Mumbai (http://dspace.library.iitb.ac.in), NIO Goa (http://drs.nio.org), NCL Pune (http://dsapce.ncl.res.in), INFLIBNET (http://www.inflibnet.ac.in/gsdl), IISc Bangalore (http://eprints.iisc.ernet.in), NAL Bangalore (http://nal-ir.res.in), NISCAIR online periodicals repository (nopr.niscair.res.in), Open MED@NIC (http://openmed.nic.in), IIM Kozhikode (http://eprints.iimk.ac.in), URDIP Pune (http://oa.csirexplorations.com/), etc.

BEST PRACTICES TO MANAGE IR

To manage IR efficiently and provide effective services using IR, librarians have to follow best practices so that sustainable IR can be developed and managed. Some of the factors to be considered are:

- Institution can select a unique institutional domain that can be used by all the websites of the institution. Well known acronyms should be used including descriptive word, like the name of the city, in the domain name

- A large web presence is made possible only with the effort of a large group of authors. One can allow a large proportion of staff, researchers or graduate students to be potential authors and maintain their own websites. A distributed system of authoring can be operative at several levels.
- Important resources in non electronic format that can be converted to web pages for easy access
- The Web (IR) is a hyper textual corpus with links connecting pages. So interlinking of WebPages need to be done properly
- Web audience is global so language should be globally accepted. All pages should be mandatory in English
- Although html is the standard format of web pages, sometimes it is better to use rich file formats like Adobe Acrobat pdf or MS Word doc as they allow a better distribution of documents. Sometimes postscript format is also difficult to open then PDF format is recommended.
- IR design may be search engine friendly so avoiding cumbersome navigation menus based on Flash, Java or JavaScript that can block the robot access is advisable.
- IR popularity and visit statistics to site has to be maintained.
- For enriching site the use of meaningful titles and descriptive Meta tags can increase the visibility of the pages. There are some standards like Dublin Core that can be used to add authoring info, keywords and other data about the web sites.
- It is necessary and mandatory to maintain a copy of old or outdated material in the site. Sometimes

relevant information is lost when the site is redesigned or simply updated and there is no way to recover easily the vanished pages.

CONCLUSION

Institutional repositories are one of the most promising developments that utilize new web technologies to offer a viable and sustainable alternative to the current model of scholarly publishing. The repositories also serve as a comprehensive publications database of the parent organization. The aim of institutional repositories is to aid the management and dissemination of the scholarly electronic resources produced by academics. ICT has transformed the scholarly environment and management of information in an academic sector viz. digital publishing and preservation, e-learning and teaching, distance education, etc. New initiatives in academic and information sector are taking place and compilation of intellectual contributions of an organization is made available in the form of IR using ICT.

Institutional Repository is an electronic archive of the scientific and scholarly outputs of an institution. IR brought grey literature in lime light. The move is now towards development of mega consortium and networking of IR. Academic institutes are managing to compile the intellectual output of the institute published in different forms like articles in journals, technical reports, processing's, historical record, manuscripts, rare collection, theses and dissertations, teaching material, research notes / data / information. Since software's like Dspace are available free it is easy to create a repository. Development of IR has emerged as new strategy in universities and research organizations and its growth is fast. IR is essential as it takes care of scholarly data and digital scholarship (DS) of the academic and research institutes.

REFERENCES

Barton Mary R. et al. (2005)., Creating an institutional repository: LEADIRS Workbook, Available at www.dspace.org/../leadirs.pdf.

Boufarss, M. (2011). If we build it, will they come? : A survey of attitudes towards institutional repositories among faculty of petroleum institute. *International journal of library science*, Vol. 3(11). Retrieved from http://www.ceser.in/ceserp/index.php/ijls/article/view/2915

Bhardwaj, Raj Kumar. (2014). Institutional repository literature: A bibliometric analysis. Science and Technology Libraries ahead-of-print pp 1-18.

Drake, M A (2004) Institutional Repositories: Hidden treasure. *Searcher*, Vol. 12(5). Accessed at http://www.infotoday.com/searcher/may04/drake.shtml

Gonzales, A. Bustos. (2007). Guidelines for the creation of institutional repositories at universities and higher education institutions. Retrieved from eprints.rclis.org/13512/2/guidelines_IR_english.pdf

Institutional Repository. Retrieved from https://en.wikipedia.org/wiki/Institutional_repository

Jain, P. et al. (2009). The role of institutional repository in digital scholarly communication. Retrieved from *http://www.library.up.ac.za/digi/docs/jain_paper.pdf.*

Johnson, R. K. (2000). Institutional repositories: Partnering with faculty to enhance scholarly communication. *D Lib Magazine*, 8(11). Retrieved from www.dlib.org/dlib/nov02/johnson/11johnson/html)

Lynch, Clifford. (2003). Institutional repositories: Essential infrastructure for scholarship in *the digital age. Portal: Libraries and the Academy, Vol. 3(2), pp 327-336.* Retrieved from http://www.arl.org/bm~doc/br226ir.pdf

Lynch, Clifford. (2003). Institutional repositories: Essential infrastructure for scholarship in *the digital age.* ARL Bimonthly Report, No. 226, Retrieved from www.arl.org/newsltr/226/ir.html.

Narayana, Poornima. (2009). Institutional repositories: An effective scholarly communication channel. Presented at National Symposium on "Open Access and Building Institutional Repositories" 21st-23rd January 2009, National Aerospace

Laboratories, Bangalore, India. Retrieved from *www.icast.org.in/nsoabir/.../IR_Scholarly_Commn_Çhannel.ppt.*

Nixon, W. (2002). The evolution of an institutional e-prints archive at university of Glasgow. *Ariadne,* no. 32 p.28 Retrieved from www.ariadne.ac.uk/issue32/eprint-archives.

PALS (2004), Pathfinder Report on Web Based Repositories, Available at www.ncsi.iisc.ernet.in/indest-ncsi.

Pickton, M. and Barwick, J. (2006). A librarians guide to institutional repositories. Retrieved from http://magpie.lboro.ac.uk/dsapce/handle/2134/1122.

Rajshekar, T. B. (2010). Institutional repositories: Vehicles for digital preservation and dissemination of organizational intellectual output. In Librarianship Today Ed. By A Gadre, and P N Rath. Pune; Diamond Publications, pp 10-24 (ISBN 978-81-8483-318-8).

Swan, Alma. (2009). Open access institutional repositories: A brieûng paper. Open Scholarship.

Westell, M. (2006). Institutional repositories: Proposed indicator of success. *Library Hi Tech,* Vol. 24 (2), pp 211-226.

8

Building An Institutional Repository : A Complete Installation Guide using SOBEKCM OSS

Ali Akbar Petiwala

INTRODUCTION

Institutional Repository is a concept for collecting, managing, publishing and preserving scholarly works created in digital form by faculty, students and researcher in individual universities, colleges and even schools. It is totally digital in nature. Apart from intellectual output, administrative documents and teaching materials coming out of the normal academic life may also be a part of IR. A single organization or multiple institutes constituting an organization can setup an IR. Its access can be open to all members or certain limitations can be defined by policy.

IR is a source for managing intellectual resources properly. Research material is hosted and managed on an IR server using special software like DSpace, Greenstone, Fedora. E-Print etc. can be accessed on the

LAN/intranet + Internet/private network.

BENEFITS OF IR

- Proper dissemination of resources leads for the long term preservation of scholarly work.
- Authors are benefited by acting as contributor.
- Institution of course can act as a sponsoring body.
- User can browse and search the documents in IR. Users can access the full/partial text as defined by policy. In case of partial access, users can avail 'Request a copy' service.
- Grey literature like teaching materials, unpublished documents can be accessed from IR.

WHAT TO UPLOAD?

- Published Research Material like Journal articles, Book chapters, Conference papers etc.
- Unpublished Research Material like preprints, working papers, Thesis/dissertations, technical reports, progress/status reports, committee reports presentations, teaching materials, audio/video clips, audio-books, e-books etc.

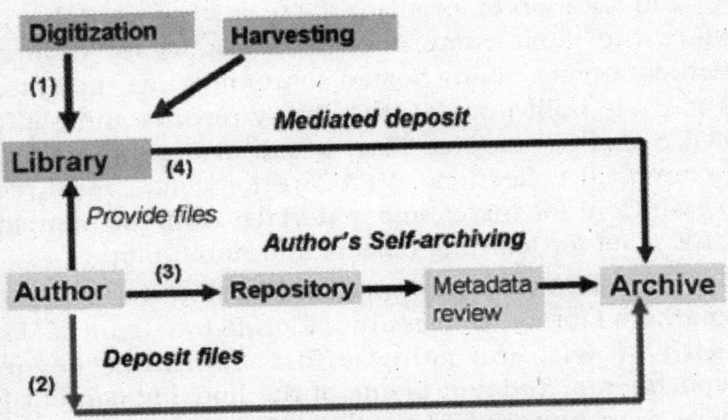

Fig. 8.1. Explains the workflow of IR works and process of archiving

SETTING UP IR USING SOBEKCM

SobekCM is the IR software engine which powers digital repositories by allowing users to discover online resources via semantic and full-text searches. For each digital resource in the repository there are a plethora of display options selected by appropriately authenticated use. It includes online metadata editing and online submission to support institutional repositories. More than just a digital repository, it's also a workflow management tool. It supports nearly all file formats for upload.

SobekCM provides a single solution for universities, colleges, museums, archives, and other heritage organizations to support the discoverability and access to digital resources and facilitate the creation of digital scholarly works. SobekCM comes with unrivalled file and metadata support. It has built-in viewers for all standard resource types from books, slides, and photographs to newspapers and electronic theses and dissertations. Multiple files are accepted without any restrictions. This flexibility, along with an innovative set of ways to hierarchically organize resources, allows complete control and customization of user's experience.

In addition to excellent file type support, SobekCM offers the most comprehensive support for different metadata types of any hosted solution. While the system is natively built upon MARC library records and METS/ MODS digital resource files, it can also support EAD's for archival collections, VRACore for visual resources, DarwinCore for taxonomic materials, GML for mapping, IEEE-LOM for learning objects and much more.

SobekCM software was developed at the George A. Smathers Library, University of Florida by a team of Mark Sullivan with on-going effort spanning several departments. Today it is one of the housing content for more than hundred institutions. It is released as OSS under the GNU GPL license and can be downloaded from the SobekCM Software Download Site.

Year	Accomplishment
2006	SobekCM First Released • Display layer over Greenstone Digital Library • Written in C#, served by Windows IIS • Based on MODS/METS
2011	Version 3.0 Released • Second major rewrite • No longer dependent on Greenstone Digital Library • Integrated tracking and workflow • SobekCM Released as Open Source
2013	Version 4.0 Released • HTML5 / CSS3 • Online Quality Control
2014	*Sobek Digital Hosting & Consulting* created to offer hosted solution

Fig. 8.2. Brief History of SobekCM Development

INSTALLING SOBEKCM ON WINDOWS 7(WIDELY USED MICROSOFT OS)

Basic Server Specifications

Since the digital repository was written in C# predominantly, it only operates under a Microsoft Windows / IIS environment to date. None of the hardware for this system needs to be particularly robust. It is recommended to have at least 4GB of memory and 80GB of disk space on the web server. Hard drive space needed for this is mostly dependent on how much full text will be uploaded.

Pre-requisite Software

Listed below is the pre-requisites software which is needed to be installed before running SobekCM setup file.

a .NET Framework Version 4.5

.Net is a new framework for developing web-based

and windows-based applications within the Microsoft environment. It's a programming infrastructure created by Microsoft for building, deploying, and running applications and services that use .NET technologies, such as desktop applications and Web services.

Link to download: *https://www.microsoft.com/en-in/download/details.aspx?id=30653*

b. Microsoft SQL Server with Full Text Searching

Microsoft SQL Server is a relational database management system (RDBMS) from Microsoft that's designed for the enterprise environment. SQL Server runs on T-SQL (Transact -SQL), a set of programming extensions from Sybase and Microsoft that add several features to standard SQL, including transaction control, exception and error handling, row processing, and declared variables. The product is said to provide enhanced flexibility, scalability, reliability, and security to database applications, and to make them easier to create and deploy, thus reducing the complexity and tedium involved in database management. SQL Server also includes more administrative support. The full-text searching components of the database must also be installed. The free version of Microsoft SQL (Express) is sufficient for smaller libraries. Ex. Microsoft SQL Server2008 R2 RTM - Express with Advanced Services.

Link to download: *http://www.microsoft.com/en-us/download/details.aspx?id=25174*

c. Internet Information Services (IIS)

IIS 7, 7.5 provides a redesigned World Wide Web Publishing Service architecture that can help to achieve better performance, reliability, scalability, and security for web sites. IIS is one of the most powerful web servers provided by Microsoft that is able to host and run web applications. It supports the following protocols: FTP, FTPS, SMTP, NNTP, HTTP/HTTPS. Web sites can be hosted on IIS; or can be used as an FTP site also. By default, IIS is not installed on Windows® 7 Professional, Enterprise, or Windows® 7 Ultimate. IIS can be install by clicking on Windows Features in Advanced Options under Programs in Control Panel. The web application requires IIS 7 or 7.5 to be installed on web server. This is included in most Window machines.

d. Java Runtime Environment (JRE)

The Java Runtime Environment (JRE), also known as Java Runtime, a set of programming tools for developing Java applications. The Java Runtime Environment provides the minimum requirements for executing a Java application; it consists of the Java Virtual Machine (JVM), core classes, and supporting files. Latest Oracle's Java Runtime Environment is a must-have installation. It's required to run several Web-based services and such software like Apache-Tomcat.

Link to download: *http://www.oracle.com/technetwork/java/javase/downloads/jre7-downloads-1880261.html*

e. Apache Tomcat

Apache Tomcat is an open source software implementation of the Java Servlet and Java Server Pages technologies. Tomcat, or officially named Apache Tomcat is a light-weight web container used for deploying and running web application based on Java. Just like apache for PHP as container, tomcat's role is becoming a runtime for java web application. There are so many web containers in the world but I choose tomcat as this tutorial since tomcat is quite easy to be understood and the server management is not that difficult. So for beginner, tomcat is a good kick-start to a real application server. For development, tomcat is a best friend since it has a very quick start-up and it's reliable for small number of applications.

(***Note:*** Apache Tomcat requires the installation of the latest Java JRE.)

Link to download: *http://www.us.apache.org/dist/tomcat/tomcat-7/v7.0.64/bin/apache-tomcat-7.0.64.exe*

f. SobekCM

SobekCM (alternately Sobek and SobekCM) is an Open Source software engine and suite of associated tools for digital libraries and digital repositories for galleries, libraries, archives, museums, colleges, universities, scholarly research projects as with the Digital Humanities, Research Data Collections, and more. SobekCM is named in part for the Egyptian crocodile god, Sobek. SobekCM's name comes in part of the mythical Sobek's role as a collector of lost things, or "the idea that as a crocodile, Sobek is the best suited to collecting items upon the Nile."

Link to download: *http://sobekrepository.org/software/download*

Please note that for security reasons, it's advisable to make at least one service/user account with password. At the time of installation, keep it handy.

Installation Steps

Name	Date modified	Type	Size
apache-tomcat-7.0.64	08/09/2015 20:19	Application	9,502 KB
dotNetFx45_Full_setup	07/09/2015 19:13	Application	982 KB
SobekCM_4_8_11_x86	07/09/2015 19:06	Windows Installer ...	48,364 KB
SQLEXPRADV_x86_ENU_2	08/09/2015 22:05	Application	7,44,882 KB

Fig. 8.3. Before attempting installation please check that all files are downloaded and saved in one folder as shown above.

Step 1. JRE

- After downloading the required software from the above given link.

- After the download is complete, click Run again.
- When the User Account Control Screen comes up, hit Continue.
- Click Next.
- Accept the license agreement by clicking Install.
- JRE is now installed.

Step 2. Microsoft .NET 4.5 Framework

- After downloading the required software from the above given link.
- After the download is complete, run the installer setup file.
- It will start downloading in-built required files from internet.
- Follow the on-screen instruction.
- .NET 4.5 is now installed.

Step 3. Microsoft IIS

- Go to [Start/Control Panel/Programs and Features]
- Click in the left panel on "Turn Windows features on or off"
- Expand "Internet Information Services" and enable these options:
- Web Management Tools, IIS6 Management Compatibility, check "II6 Scripting tools"
- Web Management Tools, IIS Management console
- Web Management Tools, IIS Management Scripts and Tools
- Web Management Tools, IIS Management Service
- At 'World Wide Web Services/ Application Development Features', enable :
- .NET Extensibility
- ASP
- ASP.NET

- At 'World Wide Web Services/Common Http features', enable:
- Static Content
- Click "OK" and let Windows update. This may take some time.

Step 4. Apache Tomcat

- Once the setup file is downloaded from the above given link, double click on "apache-tomcat-7.0.64.exe" and follow the on-screen instructions.
- While being prompted for choosing destination directory, choose the default path.
- Follow the default on-screen instruction until the installation is finished

  (***Note:*** Apache Tomcat requires the installation of the latest Java JRE.)

Step 5. Microsoft SQL Server 2008 R2 Express Edition

- Double click on the installer. It will take some time to extract. After that a window will open as follow.
- From this window click on the Installation menu (See Left). Now there will be appear some option under Installation. From right, click on the option New SQL Server stand-alone installation or add features to an existing installation.

  Note: After Clicking on that a window may appear as bellow. Just click on the button Run Program of that.
- Now setup will take a moment to complete some operation. To continue there cannot be any operation with status failed. If any operation fails then it will not be possible to continue installation. Click OK
- Check accept the terms and click NEXT
- Now Click Install button. Some setup support files will be installed.

- Now again it needs some operation to be completed. Every operation must be passed or warning or skipped. If any operation fails then it is not possible to continue. Click Next.
- Now select the features which is needed. Here I am selecting Database Engine Services, Full-Text Search Business Intelligence Development Studio, Management Tools basic & SQL 1 Client Connectivity SDK. Click Next.
- Click Next.
- Now a window will appear and it will show the space required and available. Click Next.
- Here select the account name from the dropdown list for SQL Server Database Engine-NT AUTHORITY\NETWORK SERVICE and Click Next.
- Select "mixed mode" option.
- For mixed mode I have to provide Strong password(Ex. Passw0rd!) for the root account (username "sa" default) and adding my current user by which i will also be able to access database engine without default administrator account (username : sa).
- Click Next
- Now again every operation must be passed or skipped. If there is any operation with status failed then installation will not be possible. Click Next
- Now finally it is going to start the installation. Click Install
- Now wait till installation is complete. Setup is complete. Click Next
- Now Close this window
- At last Exit this window. Installation is complete
- *If the database is on a different server, enable TCP/ IP on that server.*

Step 6. SobekCM

- After Completion of Steps (1-5), Double Click on the SobekCM.exe setup file.
- On first window simply click on next.
- Accept the terms and click on next.
- Choose Full Install option which will enable all the services and install all necessary files.
- As shown in figure 8.4, enter Computer/Database Server name and Database name.

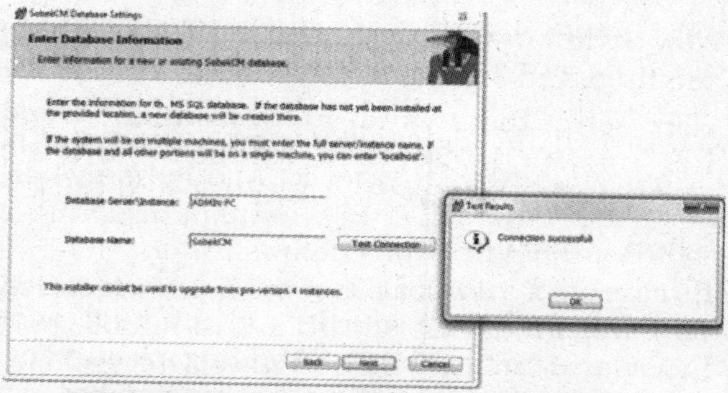

Fig. 8.4. Enable Service & Install all File

- Next screen will be as shown in figure 8.5, it indicates that previous all installation and settings were successful. Click Next.

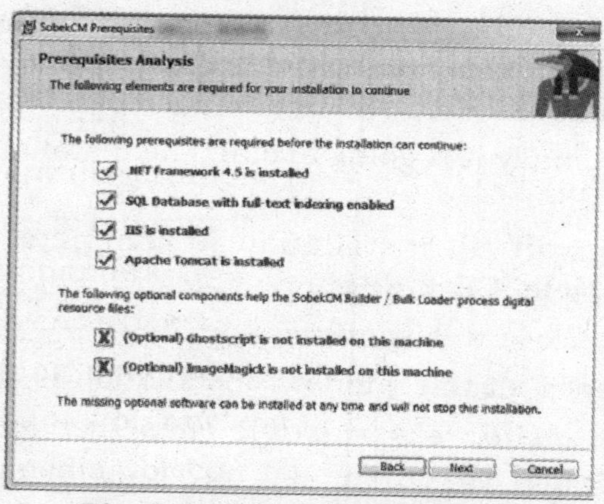

Fig. 8.5. Select Prerequisites

- On next screen, provide Institution name and its Abbreviation. Click Next.
- As shown in figure 8.6, it will prompt for system administrator account details and password. After entering. Click Next

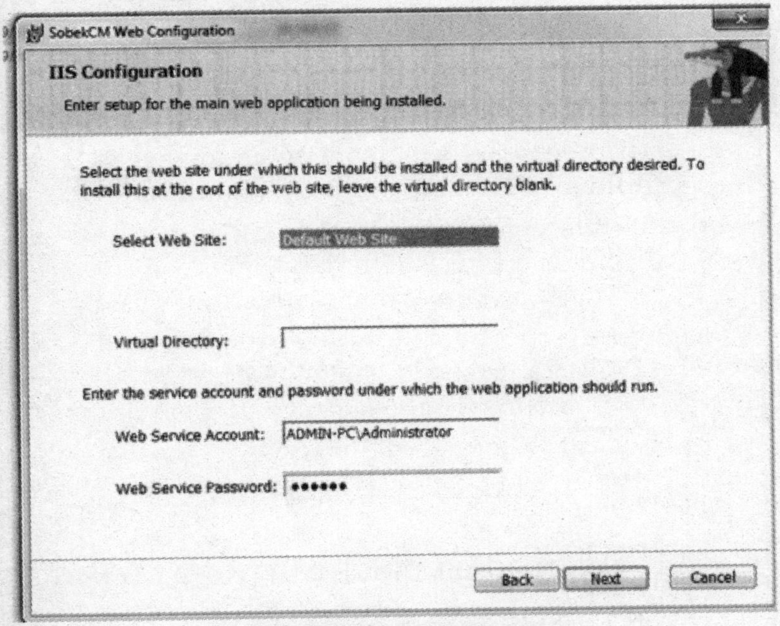

Fig. 8.6. Account Details

- On Builder Configuration screen, enter administrator account name and password.
- Click on Next and click on finish
- Launch SobekCM
  — *Finally SobekCM is installed and along with that it has created one Database which can be viewed from SQL Server Management Studio and it has also created web-based files in C:\inetpub\wwwroot.*

Working on SobekCM

- Click on Finish, it will redirect to one of default

browser with the localhost link so that it can carry out few remaining configuration like registration shown in figure 8.7 below.

- Select Register Now and registration screen will be shown. Enter personal information on the screen below and hit SAVE.

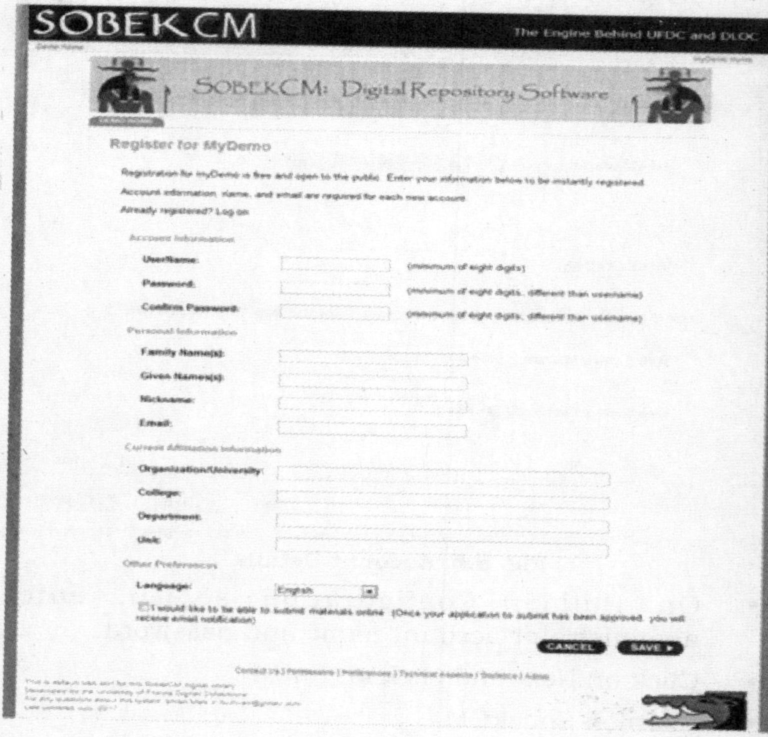

Fig. 8.7. Registration

- First launch of SobekCM repository after the registration is completed shown in figure 8

Fig. 8.8. Launch of SOBEKCM Digital Library

- Select the link in the upper right corner of the header for 'myHome'. This will bring up the login screen below in figure 8.9.

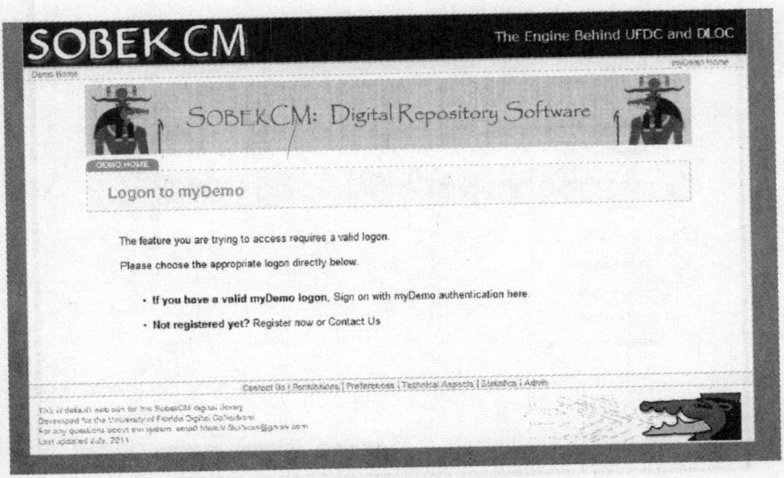

Fig. 8.9. Login page

- After logged-in, click on accept and start uploading.

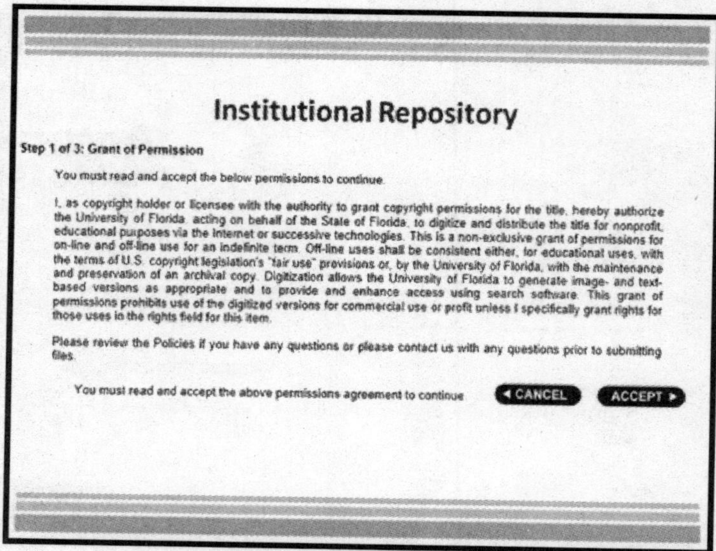

Fig. 8.10. Uploading content

- After entering required details as shown in the figure 8.11, Click Next

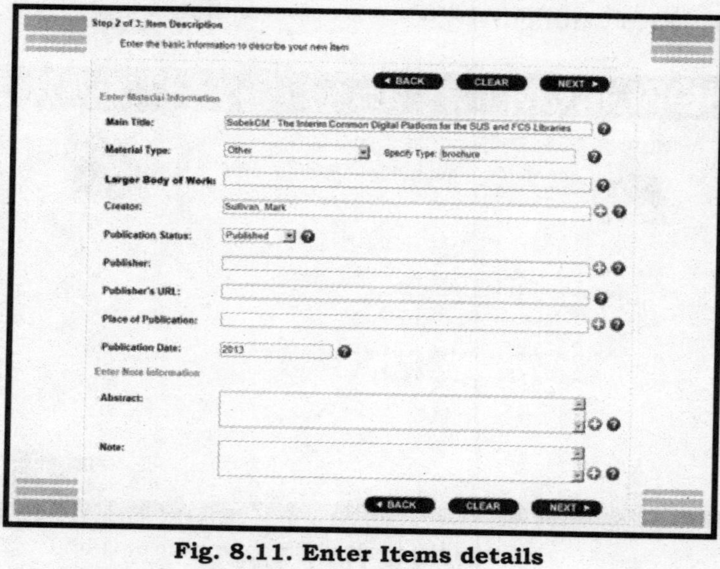

Fig. 8.11. Enter Items details

- Next screen will allow to browse any format file and

once it's done, click on upload tab. Click Finish.

- Next window will confirm that files are uploaded successfully and it can be edit or view the same files as shown in figure 8.12.

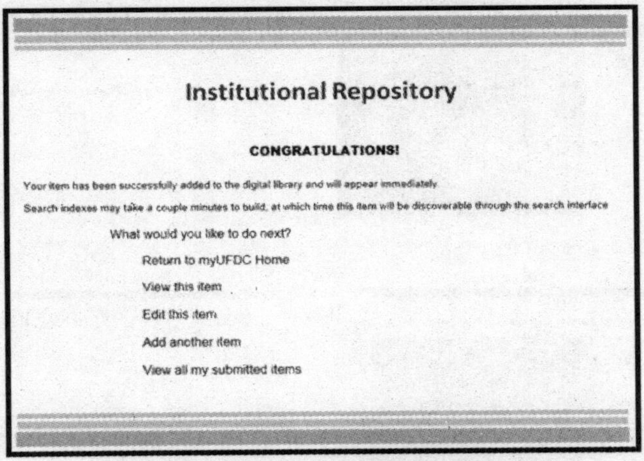

Fig. 8.12. Edit/Add/View Items

- Simultaneously subject-wise collection can be created and it will display main webpage as shown in figure 8.13.

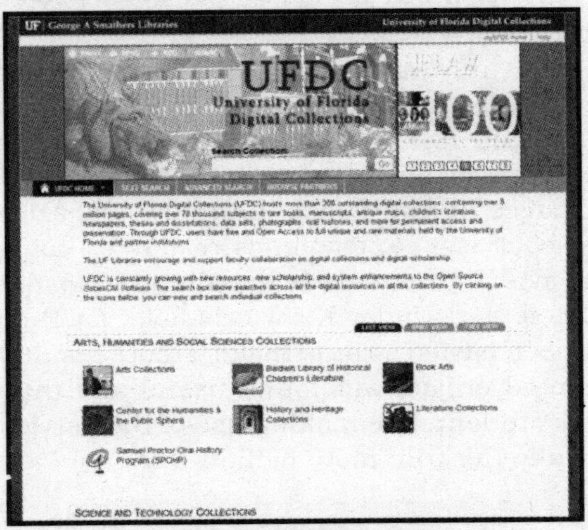

Fig. 8.13. Main web page

- Figure 8.14 shows few examples on how different file formats will come-up as an output.

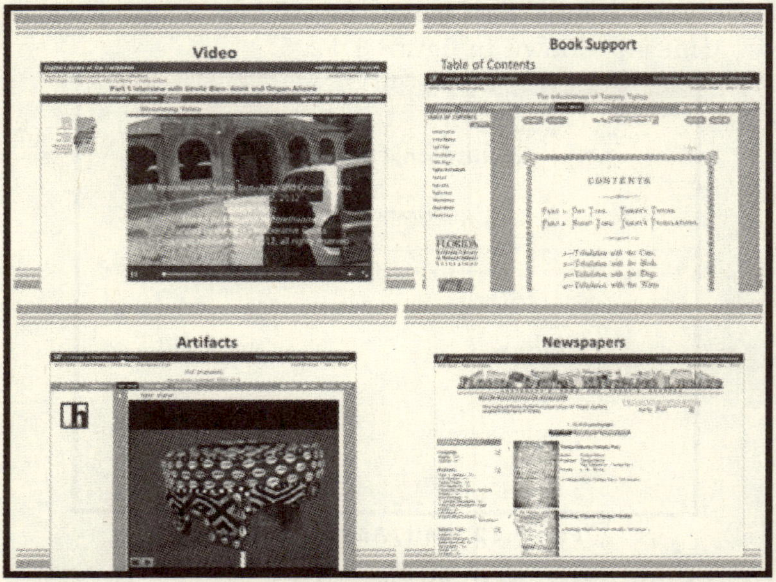

Fig. 8.14. File Formats

IMPLEMENTATION OF SOBEKCM IN SEVA SADAN B. ED COLLEGE LIBRARY

A pilot study was made to implement the said project with Seva Sadan's Library, Ulhasnagar. As the collection shown in figure 8.15, a database was created using all these resources by scanning and OCR process. The content pages of rare books, journals, magazines along with the back issues, teachings resources comprises of different media formats is scanned and uploaded on the SobekCM server. Under Keywords field, OCR converted text has been pasted so as to make it more result oriented. Implemented project was found useful and thus faculty as well as students are making use of the services which was actually the true moto behind this.

Books		23667
Titles		2198
Journals	National	24
	International	02
Magazines		04
Offline (Audio visual teaching learning) resources		88

Fig. 8.15. Seva Sadan's Library Collection

CONCLUSION

From the above guide it is concluded that building an Institutional Repository has now became a mandatory task for Libraries as technology continues to evolve exponentially and as the amount of electronic information mushrooms. An Institutional Repository is an online locus for collecting, preserving, and disseminating, in digital form, the intellectual output of an institution. Institutional Repositories represent a certain basic cost to an institution but there are ways of minimising this. A Repository that is filled by self-archiving – that is, by researchers depositing their own articles – is far less costly to an institution than one where the library does all the depositing work.

SobekCM, therefore, was designed as an open source application that institutions and organizations could run with relatively few resources. SobekCM helps the Librarians to implement IR in an easier manner because its OSS based on Windows OS. This research also concludes that Library professionals are generally facing problems while dealing with open source software based on Linux OS. Thus the SobekCM followed the librarian's inclination to create a system that would be as easy as possible to implement and use.

REFERENCES

SobekCM Website (*http://sobekrepository.org*)

9

Potential and Prospects of Traditional Knowledge Digital Library (TKDL) : A Call of Digital India

Nidhi Gauba Dhawan

INTRODUCTION

Intellectual Property Rights (IPR) are the legal rights that may be obtained for any property that arises due to intellectual efforts of an Individual or a group of individuals. Just like any other property, it can be bought, sold, traded, and licensed to others for use by its owner(s). To get the legal rights for intellectual creations, some necessary procedures are to be pursued (Puri and Viswanathan, 2009).

The laws at domestic and international levels forbid the grant of patents of traditional knowledge of any local community. Despite the fact, the traditional knowledge, including exceptional plants and their properties is being taken over by fraudulent groups by patenting them in countries other then their origin. The way to check such activities is to present prior art support demonstrating that the knowledge was previously existing and practiced (Ruiz, 2002). Therefore, the proofs existing in the form of old references/books, plays a key role in protecting the traditional knowledge. But, the additional challenge is to provide protection to the un-documented traditional knowledge that exists in ancient scripts. In some cases, the traditional knowledge is also available in the form of local legend, traditions, customs and songs, which are not properly documented (Mandal, 2008).

In recent time there has been an enormous revolution in the conventional methods of collection, storage, processing, and accessing of information. This is owing to the expansion of virtual libraries, digital libraries, online databases, and library and information networks. The recent advances in digital technology, Internet connectivity, and physical content together have resulted in a development of digital library (Varatharajan and Chandrashekara, 2007). Through these digital libraries and the digitization of print materials resources in art and culture, education, science and technology, literature and humanities, media and entertainment, and cultural heritage and history can be preserved. In India, a considerable number of libraries and information centers have commenced digital library ventures together with creation of databases and e-journals, or by digitizing their own archival-valuable compilations. In India there is a pressing need to preserve hundreds of thousands of ancient books and manuscripts, number of them still conserved in palm leaves, through digitization to protect the cultural heritage of the country (Gaur, 2009).

The call of Traditional Knowledge Digital Library (TKDL) commenced due to the legal conflict initiated by Council of Scientific and Industrial Research (CSIR) from India for the re-examination of patent No. US 5 401 504, granted to two US based Indians for the wound healing properties of turmeric. This was the first case in which a patent based on the traditional knowledge of a developing country was challenged successfully and US PTO revoked the patent (Datta and Nischal, 2010). In an another case the revocation of the patent granted to W.R. Grace Company and US Department of Agriculture on Neem (EPO patent No. 436 257) was made by European Patent Office (EPO), again on the identical grounds of its use having been recognized in India. Subsequent to these experiences of unlawful patenting, TKDL project was formally established in June 2001(Gupta, 2005).

FROM TRADITIONAL TO DIGITAL LIBRARIES

The present day change from the traditional to digital libraries not only a technological progression, but a transformation in the model by which people access and interact with information. The tools employed by librarians in their routine have changed enormously in recent time (Castelli, 2006). Today, in addition to conventional means like card catalogs and microfiche readers, the majority of the libraries now also offer an online public access catalog (OPAC), public PCs equipped with CD-ROM drives, scanners, or open terminals connected to the Internet. A growing number of libraries are creating homepages on the World Wide Web from where users have right to use to a range of services without actually entering a library (Johnson, et.al. 2008).

In present time the digitization and creation of digital libraries are vital for propagating and conserving information. The activities of digital library activities are gathering impetus in developing countries like India (Kar and Seadle, 2004). As the majority of higher education and research institutions in India are financed and controlled by the central and state governments, there is an urgent requirement of definite national plans and policies, regarding infrastructure, standards, metadata, interoperability, multi-lingual databases, training, co-ordination, copyright, and archiving and preservation methods. This would help to preserve our heritage of knowledge and culture, that would be able to survive through the destruction of time and the present as well as future generations can benefit and be steered by them (Ramdasi and Altekar 2001).

It is anticipated that digitization of libraries will continue and expand. This will result in increasing demands on the LIS professionals and Computer science professionals with superior system. Thus, will result in increased number of library departments and programmes to get into digitization. Digital libraries will expand on growth in the information and data management area. Digital libraries present an effectual means to distribute learning resources to the users. The planning of a digital library requires thoughtful analysis of the organization and its users, and an acknowledgement of the cost and the need for infrastructure and ongoing maintenance (Adams, Jansen, and Smith 1999).

TRADITIONAL KNOWLEDGE DIGITAL LIBRARY (TKDL): CONCEPTION AND DEVELOPMENT

The interaction between Intellectual Property Rights (IPR), Patent and Traditional Knowledge (TK) has become very important for its inventor and for the world's intellectual community in general. Since, the promotion of TK is now widely recognized and it also plays an important role in supporting TK-based community employment and traditions, further, the competitive business advantage and the financial affluence of knowledge holder's call for the preservation, protection and promotion of TK (Farran, 2014).

Therefore, the conservation and protection of traditional knowledge have been a matter of concern to the developing countries in general and India in particular. India has awakened to the mission of protecting her traditional knowledge from patent bio-piracy. As a result of this, in 1999, the Department of

Ayurveda, Yoga & Naturopathy, Unani, Siddha and Homoeopathy-(AYUSH), erstwhile Department of Indian System of Medicine and Homoeopathy (ISM&H) constituted an inter-disciplinary unit, for the creation of an approach paper on establishment of a Traditional Knowledge Digital Library (TKDL).

Traditional Knowledge Digital Library (TKDL), India includes about 2.08 lakh formulations based on Ayurveda, Unani, Siddha, and Yoga. These have been recorded in five different languages, namely, English, French, German, Spanish and Japanese. The objective of this is to prevent its misappropriation at the foreign patent offices. TKDL has provided access of the TKDL directory to the major Foreign Patent Offices that includes USPTO, EPO, JPO, and Canadian Patent Office (TKDL). It has been stated on the website of TKDL that approximately 75 Europeans patents and roughly a dozen USPTO patents are modified after the creation of TKDL.

The representative record of TKDL contains 1200 formulations chosen from a variety of traditional texts of natural systems of medicine (Ayurveda, Unani and Siddha. Out of these 500 formulations are from Ayurveda, Unani each and remaining 200 formulations are from Siddha (TKDL).

The TKDL project comprises of documentation of the traditional knowledge available in open/public domain in the form of Traditional Knowledge Resource Classification (TKRC). It is a novel ordered cataloging system that have systematic arrangement, dissemination and retrieval system and has been developed for approximately 25,000 subgroups besides few subgroups that was available in earlier version of the International Patent Classification (IPC), related to medicinal plants, minerals, animal resources, effects and diseases, methods of preparations, mode of administration, etc (TKDL).

The rationale of the creation of TKDL is:

- To prevent the of misuse of the gigantic Traditional Knowledge present in India's Natural system of medicines;
- To utilize the TKDL database as an important tools for carrying out advanced research for based on TK;
- To facilitate the utilization of traditional knowledge for commercial purpose with prior informed consent and access and benefit sharing agreements from the inventor and marketing agency.

The procedures for establishment of TKDL commence in the year 1999. The venture of TKDL was started in the year 2001. The major landmarks of the project are:

Table 9.1. Major Landmarks of TKDL Project

Sr. No.	*Activity*	*Period*	*Responsibility*
1.	Recognition of need of creation of Traditional Knowledge (TK) data bases and need of support to developing countries by Standing Committee on Information Technology (SCIT) of World Intellectual Property Organization (WIPO).	June, 1999	Standing Committee on Information Technologies (SCIT) and WIPO
2.	Setting up of the interdisciplinary (inter-ministerial Task Force on TKDL, consisting of experts from Department of ISM&H*, Central Council of Research in Ayurveda & Siddha (CCRAS), Banaras Hindu University (BHU), National Informatics Centre (NIC), Controller General of Patents Designs & Trade Marks (CGPDTM), etc.	Jan., 2000	Department of ISM&H
3.	Cabinet Committee of Economic Affairs (CCEA's) approval on TKDL Project.	Jan., 2001	Department of ISM&H
4.	TKDL software, specifications and design.	July, 2001	Director, NISCOM

5.	Committee of Experts recommended: (i) inclusion of approx. 200 subgroups on TK against earlier few sub-groups on medicinal plants, (ii) linking of TKRC to IPC and (iii) continuation of work on biodiversity, TK and TCE.	Feb., 2003	Director, NISCOM as the member of International Task Force
6.	Constitution of Access Policy Issue Committee (APIC).	Aug., 2002	Frame policies on accessing TKDL database
7.	Completing data abstraction work on 36,000 Ayurveda formulations for creating TKDL in five languages, i.e. English, German, Spanish, French and Japanese.	March, 2003	TKDL team of Project Assistants (IT), Ayurveda, Patent Examiners and Scientists at NISCAIR
8.	Initiation of the TKDL Unani project.	June, 2004	Department of AYUSH and NISCAIR
9.	Initiation of TKDL Ayurveda Phase II.	August, 2004	Department of AYUSH and NISCAIR
10.	Access provided to European Patent Office (EPO) to TKDL database	August, 2004	Department of AYUSH and NISCAIR
11.	Request for access to TKDL by EPO.	July, 2005	CSIR
12.	Initiation of project on TKDL Siddha.	Aug., 2005	Department of AYUSH and NISCAIR
13.	Creating of TKRC containing approx. 25,000 subgroups.	Dec., 2005	NISCAIR
14.	Inclusion of 207 subgroups, related to algae, fungi, lichens or plants or derivatives thereof used in Traditional Herbal Medicines in International Patent Classification, 8th Edition.	Jan., 2006	IPC Union, WIPO
15.	Access to TKDL database to International Patent Offices (IPOs)	June, 2006	—
16.	Request by United States Patent and Trademark Office (USPTO) for access to TKDL database and sending of Access Agreement.	Dec., 2006	CSIR
17.	Initiation of activities on creation of TKDL Yoga.	Jan., 2008	CSIR, Department of AYUSH and Morarji Desai National Institute of Yoga (MDNIY)

18.	TKDL Access Agreement concluded with European Patent Office (EPO).	Feb., 2009	CSIR
19.	Request for access to TKDL by German Patent and Trademark Office (DPMA).	March, 2009	CSIR
20.	Formal agreement to TKDL Access Agreement by USPTO.	July, 2009	USPTO
21.	Prior art evidence based on TKDL citations under Third Party observations against 35 Pipe line patent applications at EPO.	June-July, 2009	Director, TKDL
22.	TKDL Access Agreement concluded with German Patent and Trademark Office (DPMA).	Oct., 2009	CSIR
23.	TKDL Access Agreement concluded with United Kingdom Intellectual Property Office(IPO).	Feb., 2010	CSIR
24.	TKDL Access Agreement concluded with Canadian Intellectual Property Office (CIPO).	Sept., 2010	CSIR
25.	First Amending Agreement to TKDL Access Agreement with European Patent Office (EPO)	Jul, 2012	CSIR
26.	First Amending Agreement to TKDL Access Agreement with CGPDTM (Indian Patent Office)	Jul, 2012	CSIR
27.	First Amending Agreement to TKDL Access Agreement with United Kingdom Intellectual Property Office (IPO)	Jan, 2014	CSIR

* Department of ISM&H is now AYUSH Source: TKDL website

The access to the TKDL has been granted to following patent offices for carrying out prior art searches and patent examination:

- European Patent Office (February, 2009)
- Indian Patent Office (July, 2009)
- German Patent Office (October, 2009)

- United States Patent and Trademark Office (November, 2009)
- United Kingdom Intellectual Property Office (February, 2010)
- Canadian Intellectual Property Office (September, 2010)
- IP Australia (January, 2011) (Source: WIPO)

PRESERVING TRADITIONAL KNOWLEDGE OF INDIA: ROLE OF TKDL

The creation of TKDL is an effort to protect India's traditional medicine from foreign pharmaceutical companies who might try to patent such medicine.

CASE STUDY 1. Turmeric

The Importance of documentation through TKDL creation can be appreciated by the outcome of a patent application number CA2454171, filed by a US multinational firm, Metaproteomics Llc, at the Canada Intellectual Property Office (CIPO). It stated the usefulness of turmeric, apple, basil, kalamegha and licorice for the treatment of inflammation, psoriasis, gastritis and as anti-inflammatory to be novel. The Traditional Knowledge Digital Library (TKDL), presented the prior art evidences in the form of references in books from 18th century to the 20th century citing evidences that turmeric, apple, basil, kalamegha and licorice have been used alone or in combination with a few other ingredients for the treatment of inflammation, psoriasis, gastritis and as anti-inflammatory in the Indian systems of medicine. A list of books were cited as a prior art evidence. Subsequently, India was successfully able to stop the firm's bid to patent the medicinal use of turmeric. Based on TKDL evidences filed for the application no. CA2454171, CIPO stated the application as 'Dead' on 28-Sep-2012 (Hirwade, 2010).

CASE STUDY 2. Neem

In another milestone decision in May, 2000, the European Patent Office (EPO) finished a decade long conflict over the ownership rights of Neem as an anti-fungal product. A patent had been granted to the United States Department of Agriculture (USDA) and the multinational corporation W.R. Grace in 1995 for a fungicide derived from seeds of the Neem tree, a tree native to the Indian subcontinent. This resulted in a campaign in the Neem case against the US multinational was the EU Parliament's Green Party by India-based Research Foundation for Science, Technology and Ecology (RFSTE) and the International Federation of Organic Agriculture Movements (IFOAM). According to RFSTE the fungicidal qualities of the Neem tree and uses of various parts of the tree (bark, leaves, seeds, etc) had been used traditionally to make insect repellents, soaps, cosmetics, tooth cleaners and contraceptives, had been recognized in India for over 2,000 years. The recognized evidences were also presented by India previous to 1995 on use of Neem for making numerous products as well as fungicide. This was used as prior art to cancel the patent granted to USDA and W.R. Grace (Hirwade, 2010).

TKDL ROLE MODEL FOR DEVELOPING COUNTRIES

TKDL is a fruitful endeavour and has been accepted as an efficient approach for checking the award of incorrect patents by the International Patent offices. Therefore, several countries and organizations such as SAARC countries (Afghanistan, Bangladesh, Bhutan, India, Maldives, Nepal, Pakistan, and Sri Lanka), South Africa, Mongolia, Malaysia, Kenya, Thailand, African regional Industrial Property Organization are enthusiastic to replicate the TKDL model for avoiding the misappropriation of their own Traditional Knowledge (TK) (Correa, 2004). It is anticipated to provide a momentum to invention, and the expansion of natural product based medicines, which would be of huge value for the mankind.

The various activities accepted for the creation of TKDL comprises of:

- Formation of TKRC, which may be for both codified and non codified knowledge and also for Components of Biodiversity Digital Library for the SAARC countries;
- Identifications of deliverables, time frame and milestones for the TKDL project;
- Use of TKDL toolkit and adopting of technical specifications of standards for the database creation and documentation of the traditional knowledge information wherein the different methods for documenting TK have been enlisted (Gupta, 2005).

CONCLUSION

The paper concludes that documentation of Traditional Knowledge (TK) is necessary for preservation, protection & future wealth creation through TK. The rich database and information presented by India's has demonstrated to be enormously useful for research and industry, both in India and abroad. Thus, TKDL provides the rationale for combining the various documents associated to traditional knowledge in a universal language and in a simple retrieval form. It is of huge benefit in developing, promoting and utilizing the traditional knowledge further. But, there are certain concerns that need urgent attention:

- Indian TKDL is based on previously documented knowledge, but how the orally transmitted traditional knowledge would be incorporated to it.
- The documentary evidences used for TKDL are owned by all citizens of the nation but, how TK held by diverse population, even cross border communities will be integrated in TKDL.
- There is some secret traditional knowledge present

with certain indigenous communities of Indian sub-continent but, till date no effort has been made to incorporate that in TKDL.

The creation such digital libraries provide prospects as well as challenges to the library professionals and information communities. They are also a good means for the distribution and dispersal of knowledge throughout the stakeholders. The planning of a digital library like TKDL will require huge investments in terms of finances, infrastructure and organisation. But, these are not supposed to act as a barrier for the development of new products, their trade and further research. They should not hamper the mutual trust among the stakeholders. And at last these should be synchronized with internationally recognized treaties.

REFERENCES

Adams, W.J., Jansen, B.J., & Smith, T. (1999). Planning, building, and using a distributed digital library. Third International Conference on Concepts in Library and Information Science. Dubrovnik, Croatia, pp 321.

Castelli, D. (2006). Digital libraries of the future – and the role of libraries. *Library Hi Tech. 24(4),* 496-503.

Correa. C. (2004). Protecting Traditional: Lessons from National Experiences, prepared for the UNCTAD meeting, Geneva, 4-6 February, 2004, pp. 34-37.

Datta, D. & Nischal, S. (2010). Looking Back to Change Track. Published by TERI. pp-123.

Farran, S. (2014). Aid, trade and taboo: the place of indigenous traditional knowledge in development strategies: a Pacific perspective. *Development Studies Research 1(1),* 28- 41.

Gaur, R. C (2009), Preservation and Access to Indian Manuscripts. *AAMES Newsletter,* 6(2).

Gupta, V. K. (2005). Traditional Knowledge Digital Library, Sub-Regional Experts Meeting in Asia on Intangible Cultural Heritage: Safeguarding and Inventory-Making Methodologies, Asia-Pacific Cultural Centre for UNESCO (ACCU) Bangkok, 9.

Hirwade, M. (2010) *Protecting Traditional Knowledge Digitally: a Case Study of TKDL.*. In Conference National Workshop on Digitization Initiatives & Applications in Indian Context, DNC, Nagpur, (3 January 2010).

Johnson, K., Trabelsi, H., & Fabbro, E. (2008). Library support for e-learners: E-resources, eservices, and the human factors, 2nd ed. (pp. 397-418). In T. Anderson (Ed.), The theory and practice of online learning.

Kar, D.C. & M. Seadle (2004). International conference on digital libraries 2004 *Conference. Library Hi-Tech News. 21(5)*, 3–7.

Mandal, S.K. (2008) Documenting the Traditional Folk Knowledge, *Research Journal of Folkloristics. Vol. 1 (1)*, 27-34.

Puri, R.S. & Viswanathan, A. (2009) Practical Approach to Intellectual Property Rights, Delhi. Published by I. K. International Pvt. Ltd.

Ramdasi, N.R. & Altekar E. (2001) Interfacing Visual Metaphors in Indian Heritage: Puranas, In Creation and Management of Digital Resources : Caliber 2001; Inflibnet Centre, Ahmedabad, India: 46-56.

Ruiz, M. (2002) The international debate on traditional knowledge as prior art in the patent system: issues and options for developing countries. *Prior Art Manual by Centre for International environmental Law (CIEL)*, 22-25.

TKDL Retrieved from *http://www.tkdl.res.in/tkdl/langdefault/common/Home.asp?GL=Eng*

Varatharajan, N. & Chandrashekara, M. (2007). "Digital Library Initiatives at Higher Education and Research Institutions in India". *Library Philosophy and Practice* Paper no. 157. Retrieved from *http://digitalcommons.unl.edu/cgi/viewcontent.cgi?article=1158&context=libphilprac*

WIPO Retrieved from *http://www.wipo.int/portal/en/index.html*

10

Institutional Repositories-Awareness by Faculty of University of Thanjavur : A Case Study

T. Narmadha

INTRODUCTION

The IR provides a method for capturing and maintaining today's electronic detritus so that tomorrow's scholars can understand the thinking behind the published record. For the standard IRs, each and every institution should have to equip its library professionals so that they are able to cope up with the ever-growing changes in this part. In view of the above Periyar Maniammai University has undertaken to create an IR and the project is under progress. The means of disseminating scholarly content has been greatly expanded through the internet and its capabilities for immediate and broad access to information. The movement towards open access (OA) journals and repositories are prime examples of the way the academies are trying to take advantage of this technology by wider dissemination of research, making it free of charge, and attempting to reduce copyright restrictions.

Institutional Repository (IR) is able to address the challenges faced by faculty members in attempting to disseminate their research through the internet, and to utilise various forms of digital media for scholarly communication. To design and develop IR, the preliminary requirement is deposition of the contents. The main source of content for any academic IR is the faculty members. To initiate and to sustain an IR, the flow of content submission is very much important. However, it may not be generalised that the potential value of IR is not yet fully appreciated by faculty members. Although very few institutions have their own IR and only a small proportion of faculty members deposit their scholarly content into it. This low rate of faculty participation is a common phenomenon across the world, and it is a major issue for the success of those repositories.

The growth in ICT has given various methods to the libraries to create, store, maintain, access, preserve and disseminate the information to their users (Gupta, *et al.* 2013). The concept of IR is one of such methods developed by academic libraries to preserve the scientific inputs of their institution. This has helped the libraries to become the creator of the information apart from storage and dissemination. Today, where Google can store and index major portion of the information, the role of IRs cannot be neglected as the information created by an institution in the form of conference articles, some copyrighted journal articles, audio-video lectures, educational power point presentations, etc., can be searched and accessed through IRs only.

Kim (2011) states that only 40.1 % faculty members of Ewha Womens University, Korea were aware of their university's IR. He also raised two basic research questions to identify the behavioral factors that motivate or hold up the willingness of faculties to contribute scholarly content in IR:

(a) What are the factors that encourage faculty participations or willingness to participate? and (b) What are the factors hold back faculty contributions or unwillingness to participate? He identified that academic reward, professional recognition; accessibility and publicity are the factors which encourage faculty participations. Additional time, effort, and copyright issues are the factors which hold back the faculty contributions. Similarly the results of the study conducted by Abrizah (2009) reveals that only 35.9 % respondents of his survey were aware that of Malaya University initiative to prepare an IR. Whereas the survey conducted by Pelizzari (2004) reveals that 44 % of the respondents of Economics and Law subjects of the University of Brescia, Italy know about the existence of IR. But of those aware of the existence of IR, only 4 % affirmed they had already used them to deposit papers.

There are also lots of works, reveal the unwillingness to participate, like Hey (2004), Thomas & McDonald (2007), and Burn & Wilson (2008). According to their several surveys there are many reasons behind the unwillingness to participate in IR. One of the most important issues in this regard is the copyright. Traditionally, authors are required to transfer their copyright to journal publishers in return for publication of their works. This is usually the case with commercial journal publishers. Commercial publishing agreement contained among its terms the assignment of copyright to the publisher. Authors were given minimal usage right to their works. The publishing agreement expressly states that the duration of the assignment would be for the full term of the copyright (usually 70 years) plus any extensions or renewals.

The problem with this conventional publishing agreement is requiring the assignment of copyright. An alternative publishing agreement (Hey, 2004) or dual copyright allows the author of a work to grant to the publisher the rights necessary to enable the publisher to publish the work while at the same time allowing the author to retain the copyright to the work. Alternatively, an author could opt to publish his work in an OA journal that permits the author to archive his published work in an open access repository like IR. In this way, the work will be given the widest possible dissemination.

OBJECTIVES

The main objectives of this study are to know about:

- The awareness of faculty members about IR
- Their willingness to participate in IR
- Their perception about incentives of IR
- Their awareness about dual copyright or alternative publishing agreement.

METHODOLOGY

A descriptive survey method that consists of the structured questionnaire has been adopted in this study for collection of data. Selected faculty members of different departments of the Periyar Maniammai University of Thanjavur, scattered in different campuses, have been interviewed. All 27 Science and Technology departments under two Faculty Councils of Post Graduate Studies of the Periyar Maniammai University of Thanjavur have been considered for this survey. The Faculty Council for Post-Graduate studies in Engineering & Technology has 7 departments and the Faculty Council for Post-Graduate studies in Science has 20 departments.

There were 314 faculty members in all 27 departments as on June 2015. 15 % (47) of them were selected consisting both the professors and others (like Associate Professors and Assistant Professors) for this survey.

ANALYSIS & FINDINGS

Preferred Channel of Publishing (other than print)

Most of the recognised academic disciplines have their own journals and other outlets for publication, although many academic journals are somewhat interdisciplinary, and publish work under several distinct fields or subfields. There is the evolution from the print to the electronic format and now, academic publishing is undergoing major changes. In this segment, the respondents were asked about their preferred channel of publication of their scholarly contents in other than print mode (Table 10.1).

Table 10.1. Preferred channel of publication

Preferred channel	*Respondents (%)*		
	Professors	*Others*	*Total*
Personal website	1 (4.16)	2 (8.70)	3 (6.4)
Departmental website	10 (41.67)	4 (17.39)	14 (929.8)
Open access journals	13 (54.17)	17 (73.91)	30 (63.8)
Total	24 (100)	23 (100)	47 (100)

It was observed that:

(a) Most of the respondents don't have personal website, so there are little scopes to prefer it in this regards. Only 3 faculty members had their personal website.

(b) 10 (41.67 %) professors expressed their preference to publish their research materials in the departmental websites, although most of the departments have no departmental websites.

(c) Most of the respondent other than the professors (73.91 %, i.e., 17), have mentioned OA journals as their preference to publish their research materials compared to the professors in this regard (54.17 %, i.e., 13). One reason may be that the other than professors are much more comfortable in handling the electronic mode and networking system as their average age (44 years) is lower than the professors' average age (56 years) (Table 10.2).

Table 10.2. Awareness about IR

Response	*Respondents (%)*		
	Professors	*Others*	*Total*
Aware	12 (50)	12 (52.17)	24 (51.06)
Not aware	12 (50)	11 (47.83)	23 (48.94)
Total	24 (100)	23 (100)	47 (100)

RESPONDENTS' AWARENESS ABOUT IR

Faculty members' view regarding IR is one of the important factors for establishing it in that organisation. In this prospect the awareness of faculty members regarding IR is also important. It is revealed from Table 10.2 that the scenario about their awareness is not satisfactory. Just more than 50 % of them are aware about it.

It is further revealed that most of the aware respondents came to aware about it through the internet. Table 10.3 shows the detail about how the faculty members became aware about IR.

It is revealed from Table 10.3 that most of the respondents, who are aware are not dependent on librarian or library staffs in this regard. 19 (80 %) faculty members came to know about it through the internet. The percentage of other than professors is much higher than the percentages of professors in the same respect. So the library professionals should take a proactive role in awareness development on it.

Table 10.3. Medium of awareness about IR

Medium of awareness	*Respondents (%)*		
	Professors	*Others*	*Total*
Internet	66.67	91.67	79.16
Librarian	16.67	8.33	12.5
Journals	8.33	-	4.17
Other	8.33	-	4.17
Total	100	100	100

WILLINGNESS TO PARTICIPATE IN IR SYSTEM

In most of the cases the respondents were found to be confused to contribute their content to the IR of different institutes. There are several reasons for unwillingness to participate in it. One of them is the copyright issue. In this study two types of content were considered, one is post-published or previously-published articles, and another is pre -published or work-in-progress articles and have asked the respondents, which one they preferred most to contribute to IR. The results are displaying in Table 10.4 and Table 10.5.

Table 10.4. Submission of Post-published articles in the proposed IR

Willing	*Respondents (%)*		
	Professors	*Others*	*Total*
Yes	13 (54.17)	11 (47.83)	24 (51.06)
No	3 (12.5)	4 (17.39)	7 (14.89)
Not sure	8 (33.33)	8 (34.78)	16 (34.05)
Total	24 (100)	23 (100)	47 (100)

51.06 % faculty members are ready to contribute their post-published articles in the IR, in case their university mandates them to do this. But the same percentage is dropping down (19.15 %) hugely when the question arises for contributing pre-published or work-in-progress articles. They want to publish new contents in any reputed journal first. The percentage of agreed professors (54.17 %) in this regard, is much more, than the other than professors (47.83 %).

Table 10.5. Submission of Pre-published articles in the proposed IR

Willing	*Respondents (%)*		
	Professors	*Others*	*Total*
Yes	4 (16.67)	5 (21.74)	9 (19.15)
No	5 (20.83)	13 (56.52)	18 (38.30)
Not sure	15 (62.5)	5 (21.74)	20 (42.55)
Total	24 (100)	23 (100)	47 (100)

INCENTIVES OF IR

There are many benefits that IR holds for academic institutions and their faculty members. It provides institutions with the opportunity to collect, store and disseminate institutional intellectual output, bring visibility to the university as well as individual faculty. In this survey option of eight different incentives of IR were given to the respondents. These are:

(a) It increases professional visibility

(b) It measures of faculty performance

(c) It improves scholarly communication

(d) It is easy to use

(e) It is a permanent place for scholarly content

(f) It support class room teaching

(g) It display intellectual achievement of the institute

(h) It provide easy access of gray literature

However, the respondents opted for only five such incentives, as mentioned in Table 10.6. 54.17 % professors and 65.22 % other than professors think the professional visibility as the most important benefit of an IR then came the intellectual achievement of the institute.

Table 10.6. Incentives of IR according to the respondents

Incentives through IR	*Respondents (%)*		
	Professors	*Others*	*Total*
Increase professional visibility	13 (54.17)	15 (65.22)	28 (59.57)
Display Intellectual achievement of the instt.	5 (20.83)	3 (13.04)	8 (17.02)
Improve scholarly communication	3 (12.50)	3 (13.04	6 (12.77)
Measure faculty performance	2 (8.33)	2 (8.70)	4 (8.51)
Support class room teaching	1 (4.17)	—	1 (2.13)
Total	24 (100)	23 (100)	47 (100)

Hence, it may be concluded that faculty members are very much interested in their professional visibility. The professors and the other than professors are more or less in the same view in these regards.

AWARENESS ABOUT DUAL COPYRIGHT OR ALTERNATIVE PUBLISHING AGREEMENT

The issues of copyright and dual copyright have already been emphasised. Copyright is the authors control over the content but this right is generally transferred to the publisher with the consent for publication through any publishing channel. Dual copyright at the same time allows the author to retain the copyright to the work. In this survey the awareness about dual copyright issue among the faculty members under study was examined.

According to Table 10.7 it is revealed that one fourth of respondents were aware about the dual copyright issues. Both the professors and other than professors are more or less on the same level in this regard. Faculties who don't want (or not sure) to contribute their content in IR have fear about copyright issue.

Table 10.7. Awareness about dual copyright among the faculty members

Dual copyright	*Respondents (%)*		
	Professors	*Others*	*Total*
Aware	5 (20.83)	4 (17.39)	9 (19.15)
Not aware	19 (79.17)	19 (82.61)	38 (80.85)
Total	24 (100)	23 (100)	47 (100)

CONCLUSIONS

Faculty's attitude towards IR is generally positive. Regarding the awareness of IR, it was found that half of the respondents are positive. Overall, the findings showed that incentive factors are more influential for participation in IR. Any form of awareness programme in this regard would be beneficial in increasing the interest to participate. Faculty members who are willing to contribute to the IR in future realised potential benefits they could get in contributing their contents in this regard.

The copyright issue is the most influential factors in regard to the unwillingness of the contribution. Most of the faculty respondents are unaware about dual copyright or dual licensing policies of the publishers. According to the faculty members all the copyright issues, including the dual copyright or multi licensing policy should be handled by the Periyar Manaimmai University authorities. That is why they are in favour of 'Mediated deposit service model', i.e., the agencies interested in establishment or maintain an IR must prepare an appropriate licensing policy in this regard. There are many IR in action but the licensing policy is in a void situation as far as Indian conditions are concerned.

REFERENCES

Gupta, Sushma; *et al.* (2013). Institutional digital repositories in India: Growth and development. *In* ILA 2013: Next Generation Libraries: New Insights and Universal Access to Knowledge. Paper presented at the 58th Indian Library Association International Conference, 27-29 February 2013, (pp. 462-71) Dharwad; Karnataka University.

Kim, J. (2011). Motivations of faculty self-archiving in institutional repositories. *J. Acad. Lib.*, Vol,37(3). Retrieved from *http://www.sciencedirect.com/science/*article/pii/S0099133311000310/

Abrizah, A. (2009). The cautious faculty: Their awareness and attitudes towards institutional repositories. *Malaysian J. Lib. & Inf. Sci.*, Vol.14(2). Retrieved from *http://umrefjournal.um.edu.my/filebank/published_* article/2392/746.pdf/

Pelizzari, E. (2004). Academic authors and open archives: A survey in the social science field. *Libri*, Vol.54, 113-22. Retrieved from *www.librijournal.org/pdf/2004-2pp113*-122.pdf/

Hey, J. (2004). Targeting academic research with Southampton's institutional repository: E-prints soton' as the university of southampton research repository. *Ariadne*, No.40. Retrieved from http://www.ariadne.ac.uk /issue40/hey/intro.html/

Thomas, C. & McDonald, R.H. (2007). Measuring and comparing participation patterns in digital repositories. *D-lib Magazine*, Vol.13(9/10). Retrieved from *http://www.dlib*.org/dlib/september07/mcdonald/09mcdonald.html/

Burn, K.L. & Wilson, K. (2008).Build it and they will come?: Assessing the impact of 'academic-friendly' practices on institutional repository growth at Southern Cross University, paper presented at Information Online 2009 Conference, Sydney, NSW, 20-22 January.

Dutta, G. (2012). Study of faculty awareness about institutional digital repository and its related issues in University of Calcutta. (M.Phil Dissertation) Department of Library & Information Science, University of Calcutta, Kolkata.

11

Indian ETD Repositories in *Open* DOAR: An Observation

Jyotshna Sahoo

INTRODUCTION

India has a great tradition of learning and has one of the largest educational systems in the world. The number of Universities in India has increased 34 times from 20 in 1950 to 677 in 2014. The higher education sector boasts of 45 Central Universities, 318 State Universities, 185 State Private universities, 129 Deemed to be Universities, 51 Institutions of National Importance (established under Acts of Parliament) under MHRD and four Institutions established under various State legislations (Department of Higher Education, MHRD GoI). Doctoral researches are considered as essential programmes for the development of higher education where universities are the key players in carrying out the major responsibility for producing good researchers and becoming a platform for generation of new research output. Doctoral research comprises one sub set of research for which India annually invests substantial resources. The doctoral researches are represented through dissertations submitted to Universities for the award of doctoral degree (Ph.D).

Theses and dissertations contribute considerably to the scholarly knowledge bank and constitute a pivotal segment of research literature. Theses submitted in support of a Ph.D. are difficult to access, as they are only collected by the library of the university that granted the degree and are not generally issued outside the university library. The results of our doctoral research have not yet received due attention in further research and application, for which doctoral research in India faces a serious handicap. There is also a danger of duplication of research. Considering the importance of doctoral theses as the primary and the unique source of scholarly communication and to overcome the disadvantage of "poor visibility" of Indian doctoral research, during the last few years more and more research and development institutions and universities are beginning to embrace the idea of creating and maintaining a repository of electronic theses and dissertations known as ETDs. In the given context the present paper examines the current ETD repositories of Indian Scenario with reference to "*Open*DOAR"- the directory of open access repositories hosted byUniversity of Nottingham, United Kingdom.

OBJECTIVES OF THE STUDY

The basic purpose of this paper is to provide the state-of-the art of Institutional Repositories enlisted in *Open*DOAR in the context ofIndia. However the study has been carried out with the following objectives:

- To find out the number of ETD Repositories from India enlisted in *Open*DOAR;
- To study the types of Institutes and the percentage of contribution on the basis of size of contents ;
- To find out the kinds of softwares used by the Indian Theses Repositories and the percentage of items digitized using those softwares;

- To reflect the top ten Organizations from India enlisted in *Open*DOAR.

SCOPE OF THE STUDY

The scope of any investigation identifies the boundaries of the study in terms of the subject coverage, objectives, area, time frame and the core issues to which the work is focused. Though *Open*DOAR is a listing of open access repositories around the world, for the present study the scope is limited to two aspects. While geographically the study is limited to the country of *India*, content wise it is confined to the study of *E-theses repositories*.

WHAT IS *OPEN*DOAR?

*Open*DOAR is an authoritative directory of academic open access repositories. *Open*DOAR provides a quality-assured, comprehensive and authoritative listing of institutional and subject-based repositories around the world .*Open*DOAR staff harvest and assign metadata to allow categorization and analysis to assist the wider use and exploitation of repositories. Each of the repositories has been visited by *Open*DOAR staff to ensure a high degree of quality and consistency in the information provided. *Open*DOAR is one of the SHERPA Services including RoMEO and JULIET,basedat the Centre for Research Communications (CRC).Current development work is currently funded by Joint Information Systems Committee (JISC), with contributions from CRC-the host organisation, the University of Nottingham. *Open*DOAR is primarily a service to enhance and support the academic and research activities of the global community. This directoryprovides search for repositories and repository contents and aims to:

- Survey the growing field of academic open access research repositories and categorise them in terms of locale, content and other measures.

- Produce a descriptive list of open access repositories of relevance to academic research.
- Provide a comprehensive & authoritative list for end users wishing to find particular types of, or specific repositories.
- Deliver a comprehensive, structured and maintained list with clear update and self-regulation protocols to enable development of the list.
- Play a prominent international role in the organisation of and access to open access repository services.
- Support Open Access outreach and advocacy endeavours within institutions and globally.

REVIEW OF LITERATURE

A set of relevant literature consisting of scholarly articles published in various established national and international journals have been reviewed for the present study. All the relevant literature have been retrieved searching through Google search engine by giving a combination of keyword options on ETD and *Open*DOAR and the reviews are given in a chronological succession:

Das, Sen & Dutta (2007)explored the policy frame works, strategic dimensions and analyses SWOT (strengths, weaknesses, opportunities and threats)of existing ETD initiatives in India. The authors mentioned about the working of the Vidyanidhi project, INDEST Consortium, CSIR and INFLIBNET Centre towards implementation of open access ETD and/or bibliographic databases of theses and dissertations. Sengupta (2012) provided a holistic view of the E-Theses repositories in World with specific referenceto India, basing on the data mainly collected from the Registry of Open Access Repositories (ROAR) and the Directory of Open Access Repositories (OpenDOAR).

Kharpade & Ambedkar (2014) discussed about the growth and the development and the history of ETD activities in India. The paper also reflected the National Policy framework in India for building ETD repositories including UGC Regulations 2005 and 2009, INDEST Consortium, ICSSR – NASSDOC and the guidelines of National Knowledge Commission to improve the quality of research and also to provide world wide access to research under open access. Moulaison, Dykas and Gallant (2015) reported the results of a nation-wide survey conducted on metadata practices among United States-based OpenDOAR repositories. Examining the repository systems and current practices of metadata in these repositories, researchers collected and analyzed the responses of 23 repositories. Results from this survey include information about the creators of metadata, best practices and resources, and controlled vocabularies. Findings of the study reflected about the current state of repository and metadata choices in open repositories in the United States.

METHODOLOGY FOR DATA COLLECTION

The information on E-Theses repositories of India was mainly collected from the Directory of Open Access Repositories (OpenDOAR) available at the site http://www.opendoar.org. A search in OpenDOAR on the basis of content (Theses) and Country (India) generated a detailed list of 35 E-theses repositories as on 1st August 2015.

ANALYSIS AND OBSERVATION

On the basis of the data collected, it is observed that 35 repositories from India are represented in OpenDOAR (Appendix 11.1). These repositories are from a host of Indian institutions both at national and institutional level as reflected in Table 11.1.

Table 11.1. Types of Institutes represented in OpenDOAR

Sl. No.	*Type Of Institute*	*No. of Institutes*	*No. of Items*	*% of Items*
1	Research Institutes	16	44333	23.5
2	Universities	10	30663	16.3
3	National Repositories	3	92077	48.9
4	IIMs	2	13018	6.9
5	IIT	2	3833	2.0
6	IIS	1	2372	1.3
7	NIT	1	2087	1.1
Total		35	188383	100

The National level initiatives are *"Shodhganga"*, *"Vidyanidhi"*and *"KrishiKosh"* while institutional level initiatives are made from Research Institutes, Universities and other national reputed institutes like IIMs, IIT,IIS and NIT. *Shodhaganga* stands for the reservoir of Indian intellectual output stored in a repository hosted and maintained by the INFLIBNET Centre, *Vidyanidhi*(Meaning 'Treasure of Knowledge' in Sanskrit) is India's premier Digital library initiative to facilitate the creation, archiving and accessing of doctoral theses hosted by University of Mysore and *KrishiKosh* is the Institutional Repository of Indian National Agricultural Research System. It is found that highest percentages (48.9%) of contributions to OpenDOAR are made from National level institutions followed by Research Institutes (23.5%) and Universities (16.3%). But the numbers of research institutions are more in numbers (16) in comparison to other types of institutes.

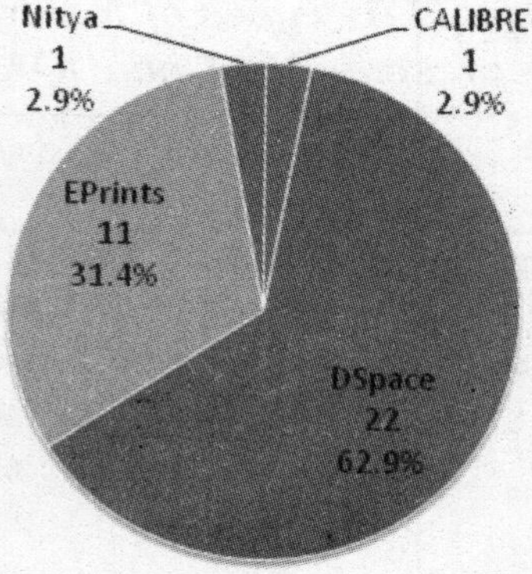

Fig. 11.1. Software used by Institutes

It is reflected from the above figure that a number of softwares namely Nitya, CALIBRE, Dspace and EPrints are currently being used for development of Indian ETD repositories. Dspace has made a mark among other institutional repositories as highest percentages (62.9%) of institutions have used this software followed by Eprints (31.4%). Nitya is used by Mahatma Gandhi University, Kerala (2.9%) and CALIBRE by Social Science Cyber Library (2.9%).

The data as regards to the number of items digitized by different software presented in figure 11.2. It is observed that highest percentage (76%) of items (theses, articles, conference proceedings, books, patents, multimedia objects) have been digitized using *Dspace* software followed by *Eprints*(15%) and *CALIBRE* (8%). This shows the popularity of Dspace among other softwares, as an Open Archives Initiative protocol for Metadata Harvesting (OAI-PMH) compliant Institutional Repository software.

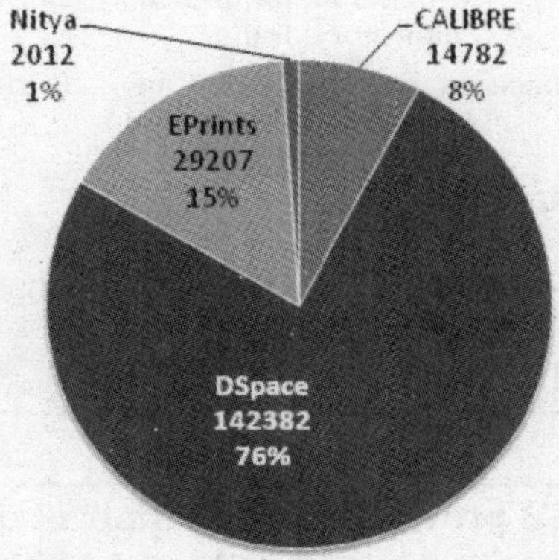

Fig. 11.2. Items digitized by different Softwares

Table 11.2. Top ten Repositories from India in OpenDOAR

Sl. No.	*Name of the Repository*	*Name of The Organization*	*Software Used*	*Items*	*%*
1	KrishiKosh	Indian Council for Agricultural Research (ICAR), India	DSpace	51326	27.2
2	ShodhGanga: A reservoir of Indian theses	Information and Library Network Center (INFLIBNET), India	DSpace	35269	18.7
3	Social Science Cyber Library	Department Of Library & Information Science, Aligarh Muslim University India.	CALIBRE	14782	7.8
4	Institutional repository@VSL	Indian Institute of Management, Ahmedabad, India	DSpace	12455	6.6
5	Eprints@CMFRI (CMFRI Digital Repository)	Indian Council of Agricultural Research (ICAR), Central Marine Fisheries Research Institute (CMFRI), India	EPrints	10108	5.4
6	DigitalLibrary@ CUSAT	CUSAT (Cochin University of Science and Technology), India	DSpace	7132	3.8
7	Indian Institute of Astrophysics Repository (DSpace@IIA)	Indian Institute of Astrophysics, India	DSpace	6484	3.4

8	Eprint@NML	National Metallurgical Laboratory, India	EPrints	5983	3.2
9	National Aerospace Laboratories Institutional Repository (NAL Repository)	Information Centre for Aerospace Science and Technology (ICAST), India	EPrints	5867	3.1
10	DSpace at Vidyanidhi	University of Mysore	DSpace	5482	2.9
		Others (25 Insitutions)		33495	17.8
		Total		188383	100

Table 11.2 provides information about the top ten institutional repositories contributed to *Open*DOAR. It is reflected that "KrishiKosh"-an institutional repository under National Agricultural Research System (NARS) tops the list with highest percentage of items (27.2%), followed by Shodhganga (18.7%),and Social Science Cyber Library (7.8%). The top ten repositories collectively contribute 82% of items where as the other 25 repositories have a share of only (18%) in *Open*DOAR. Along with ETDs, these repositories also containarticles, conference proceedings, books, patents, multimedia objects etc.

CONCLUSION

Research is considered to be the foundation for future investigation in any field of knowledge. Universities and research laboratories contribute a major role in shaping the research and development works in the areas of interest. The purpose of the research is to expand the horizons of Knowledge for the all round development of the society. Today research and development are deliberate and planned activities undertaken to create the wealth of knowledge. Both government and private industries are investing in this activity for creating new knowledge for the benefit of the society.

According to Bhartrihari, the famous Indian Sanskrit author, "Knowledge is a source that grows with sharing and decays by not sharing". Hence, the commendable efforts made by the Indian ETD repositories at different levels to make available the Ph.D. theses in open access to the entire scholarly community will certainly prove the quality and relevance of Indian doctoral research. The Online availability of electronic theses through centrally-maintained digital repositories will not only ensure easy access and archiving of Indian doctoral theses but also help in raising the standard of research.

REFERENCES

Das, A. K., Sen, B. K., & Dutta, C. (2007). ETD Policies, strategies and initiatives in India: a Critical Appraisal. In: ETD 2007: Added values to e-theses. Uppsala, 13-16 June 2007. Retrieved from *http://eprints.rclis.org/9944/*

Heather, H. L., Dykas, F. & Gallant, K. (2015). OpenDOAR repositories and metadata practices. *D-Lib Magazine,* 21 (3/4), DOI: 10.1045/march2015-moulaison. Retrieved from *http://www.dlib.org/dlib/march15/moulaison/03moulaison.print.html.*

Higher Education, Ministry of Human Resource Development, Government of India. Annual Report 2014-15 Retrieved from *http://mhrd.gov.in/sites/upload_files/mhrd/files/document-reports/Part1.pdf*

Indian ETD Repository @ INFLIBNET. (n.d.). Retrieved from *http://shodhganga.inflibnet.ac.in/*

Khaparde,V. & Ambedkar, B. (2014). Growth and development of electronic theses and dissertation (ETDs) in India. *Journal of Library & Information Science,* 2(1), 99-116.

KrishiKosh, Retrieved from *http://krishikosh.egranth.ac.in/*

OpenDOAR. Directory of Open Access Repositories. (n.d.). Retrieved from *http://www.opendoar.org/*

Sengupta, S. (2012). Status of E-theses repositories with special reference to India. *Library Philosophy and Practice,* Paper No.764. Retrieved from *http://digitalcommons.unl.edu/cgi/viewcontent.cgi?article=1838&context=libphilprac*

APPENDIX 11.1

Name Of The Repository	*Name Of The Organization*	*Software Used*	*Size*	*Subject*	*Content*
ARIES, Digital Repository	Aryabhatta Research Institute of Observational Sciences Digital Repository, ARIES, India	DSpace	807	Physics and Astronomy	Articles; Conferences; Theses; Unpublishe
DigitalLibrary@CUSAT	CUSAT (Cochin University of Science and Technology), India	DSpace	7132	Multidisciplinary	Articles; Conferences; Theses; Books; Learning Objects; Multimedia; Special
DIR@IMTECH	CSIR-Institute of Microbial - Technology (Council of Scientific and Industrial Research	EPrints	1445	Multidisciplinary	Articles; References; Theses
DRS at National Institute Of Oceanography (DRS@nio)	NICMAS (NIO library), National Institute Of Oceanography (NIO), India	DSpace	4684	Science General; Technology General; Arts and Humanities General	Articles; Conferences; Theses
DSpace @ GGSIPU	Guru Gobind Singh Indraprastha University	DSpace	135	Multidisciplinary	Articles; Theses; Learning Objects

dspace @ sdmcet	SDM College Of Engineering and Technology Dharwad, India	DSpace	60	Chemistry & Chemical Technology; Technology General; Civil Engineering; Computers and IT; Electrical and Electronic Engineering; Mechanical Engineering and Materials; Library and Information Science	References; Theses; Unpublished; Books; Learning Objects
DSpace at Indian Institute of Management Kozhikode (DSpace@IIMK)	DSpace at Indian Institute of Management Kozhikode (DSpace@IIMK)	Dspace	563	Ecology and Environment; Health & Medicine; Computers and IT; Social Sciences General; Business and Economics; Education; Management and Planning; Psychology	Articles; Conferences; Theses; Unpublished

DSpace at M S University	Smt. Hansa Mehta Library, Maharaja Sayajirao University of Baroda,	DSpace	480	Multidisciplinary	Theses
DSpace at Vidyanidhi	University of Mysore	DSpace	5482	Multidisciplinary	Theses
Dspace@NITR	National Institute of Technology, Rourkela (NITR), India	DSpace	2087	Multidisciplinary; Chemistry and Chemical Technology; Physics and Astronomy; Mechanical Engineering and Materials	Articles; Conferences; Theses; Books
DSpace@TU	Thapar University (TU), India	DSpace	3150	Multidisciplinary	Articles; Conferences; Theses
Dyuthi (Digital repository of Cochin University of Science & Technology)	Cochin University of Science & Technology (CUSAT), India	DSpace	4048	Multidisciplinary	Articles; Theses; Learning Objects
Electronic Theses and Dissertations at Indian Institute of Science (edt@IISc)	Indian Institute of Science (IISc), India	DSpace	2372	Multidisciplinary	Theses
Eprint@NML	National Metallurgical Laboratory, India	EPrints	5983	Chemistry and Chemical Technology; Technology General	Articles; Conferences; Theses; Books; Learning Objects; Patents

Eprints @MDRF	Madras Diabetes Research Foundation, India	EPrints	747	Health and Medicine	Articles; Theses; Books
Eprints@CMFRI (CMFRI Digital Repository)	Indian Council of Agricultural Research (ICAR), Central Marine Fisheries Research Institute (CMFRI), India	EPrints	10108	Agriculture, Food and Veterinary; Biology and Biochemistry; Ecology and Environment; Health and Medicine	Articles; Conferences; Theses; Unpublished; Books; Patents
Eprints@IARI	Indian Agricultural Research Institute (IARI), India	EPrints	230	Agriculture, Food and Veterinary	Articles; Conferences; Theses; Unpublished
EPrints@IITD	Indian Institute of Technology, Delhi (IITD), India	DSpace	2619	Multidisciplinary	Articles; Theses
Etheses - A Saurashtra University Library Service	Saurashtra University, India	EPrints	1064	Multidisciplinary	Articles; References; Theses
IACS Institutional Repository	Indian Association for the Cultivation of Science, India	DSpace	622	Science General	Articles; Theses; Unpublished
Indian Institute of Astrophysics Repository (DSpace@IIA)	Indian Institute of Astrophysics, India	DSpace	6484	Physics and Astronomy	Articles; Theses; Multimedia; Special
Institutional Repository of Intellectual Contributions of Delhi Technological	Delhi Technological University, India	DSpace	841	Chemistry and Chemical Technology; Mathematics	Articles; Theses; Multimedia

University				and Statistics; Physics and Astronomy; Technology General; Civil Engineering; Computers and IT; Electrical and Electronic Engineering; Mechanical Engineering and Materials	
Institutional Repository@CSIO	CSIR-Central Scientific Instruments Organisation (CSIR-CSIO), India	EPrints	359	Biology and Biochemistry; Chemistry and Chemical Technology; Earth and Planetary Sciences; Physics and Astronomy; Technology General; Computers and IT; Electrical and Electronic Engineering; Mechanical Engineering and	Articles; Conferences; Theses; Unpublished; Learning Objects; Multimedia; Special

				Materials; Management and Planning	
Institutional repository@VSL	Indian Institute of Management, Ahmedabad, India	DSpace	12455	Multidisciplinary	Articles; Conferences; Theses; Unpublished; Multimedia
Kautilya Digital Repository at IGIDR (Kautilya@igidr)	Indira Gandhi Institute of Development Research (IGIDR), India	DSpace	249	Multidisciplinary	Conferences; Theses; Unpublished
Knowledge Repository Open Network	Department of Library & Information Science, University of Kashmir, India	DSpace	1007	Science General; Agriculture, Food and Veterinary; Health and Medicine; Technology General	Articles; Conferences; Theses
KrishiKosh	Indian Council for Agricultural Research (ICAR), India	DSpace	51326	Agriculture, Food and Veterinary	Articles; Conferences; Theses; Unpublished; Books; Learning Objects; Multimedia
Librarians' Digital Library (LDL)	Documentation Research and Training Centre (DRTC), Indian Statistical Institute, Bangalore Centre (ISI), India	DSpace	510	Library and Information Science	Articles; Conferences; Theses; Multimedia
Mahatma Gandhi University Theses Online	Mahatma Gandhi University,	Nitya	2012	Multidisciplinary	Theses

National Aerospace Laboratories Institutional Repository (NAL Repository)	Information Centre for Aerospace Science and Technology (ICAST), India	EPrints	5867	Mathematics and Statistics; Technology General; Mechanical Engineering and Materials	Articles; Conferences; Theses; Unpublished; Learning Objects; Multimedia; Patents
NIRT Institutional Repository (EPrints@NIRT)	National Institute for Tuberculosis Research, India	EPrints	831	Biology and Biochemistry; Health and Medicine	Articles; References; Conferences; Theses; Books
RAIITH	Research Archive of Indian Institute of Technology Hyderabad (RAIITH)	EPrints	1214	Technology General	Articles; Conferences; Theses; Books
RAIITH	Insitute of Technology, Hyderabad, India	EPrints	1359	Technology General	Articles; Conferences; Theses; Books
ShodhGanga: A reservoir of Indian theses	Information and Library Network Center (INFLIBNET), India	DSpace	35269	Multidisciplinary	Theses
Social Science Cyber Library	Department Of Library & Information Science, Aligarh Muslim University India.	CALIBRE	14782	Social Science General	Articles, Theses, Books

(Indian ETD Repositories in *Open*DOAR)

12

Initiatives of Digital Library Projects in India, UK and USA : An Overview

Syeda Sarwat Farheen

INTRODUCTION

Information Technology is changing whole world creating new challenges and opportunities. Today libraries are surrounding by digitized data that is connected to each other through telecommunication devices. As a result of ICT the libraries changed its platform, giving rise to rich concepts such as DL-Digital literacy, KM-Knowledge Management, IL-Information Literacy, IR-Information Repositories, and archiving of culture and heritage. In India ICT concentrated mainly in institutes such as IIT's, IIM's, IISC, research institutes and some special libraries, some government agencies and public sector institutions. Whereas, the situation in developed country is different as most of the institutions are funded by the governments or private agencies to initiate institutional repository projects.

HISTORY OF DIGITAL LIBRARY INITIATIVES

The Digital Library Initiatives (DLI) began in late 1980s with discussions between researchers and agencies. The discussion progressed to planning workshops designed to develop research value and culminated in the National Science Foundation (NSF)/ Defense Advanced Research Projects Agency (DARPA)/ National Aeronautics and Space Administration (NASA) Research in Digital Libraries Initiative announced in late 1993. With the selection and funding of the six DLI projects interest and activities related to digital libraries accelerated rapidly. The six DLI projects became highly visible and influential–and grew in scope, participation and influence NSF and DARPA funded additionally. These six heralded the beginning of "digital library" initiation in India.

DIGITAL LIBRARY INITIATIVES IN USA

The Digital library Initiatives of USA has been described below phase wise.

Digital Library Phase - I

In Digital Libraries Initiative phase - I there were six federally funded projects in digital library research, with partnerships led by universities. The individual projects are listed below.

- University of California, Berkeley : An Electronic Environmental Library Project.
- University of California, Santa Barbara: The Alexandria Project: - Towards a Distributed Digital Library with Comprehensive Services for Images and Spatially Referenced Information.
- Carnegie Mellon University: Informedia:- Integrated Speech, Image and Language Understanding for Creation and Exploration of Digital Video Libraries
- University of Illinois at Urbana-Champaign:-

Building the Interspace: Digital Library Infrastructure for a University Engineering Community.

- University of Michigan:-The University of Michigan Digital Library Project.
- Stanford University:- Stanford University Digital Libraries Project.

The Digital Library Initiative Phase-II

The Digital library Initiative Phase - II is an interagency program sponsored by the;

- National Science Foundation (NSF)
- Defence Advanced Researched Projects Agency (DARPA)
- National Library of Medicine (NLM)
- Library of Congress (LOC)
- National Endowment for the Humanities (NEH)
- National Aeronautics & Space Administration (NASA)
- Federal Bureau of Investigation (FBI)

PILOT PROJECTS IN USA

The Alexandria Project (*http://alexandria.ucsb.edu/*)

The Alexandria Digital Research Library (ADRL) is UC Santa Barbara Library's home. The UCSB developed in the 1990s with the Alexandria digital Library, the new ADRL will be a comprehensive digital library featuring unique research texts, data, images, maps, and audio and video recordings. ADRL launched in April 2014, with its first collection: electronic theses and dissertations by UCSB students.

Computer Science Technical Report (CS-TR) Project (*https://www.cs.princeton.edu/reasearch/techreps*)

"The Computer Science Technical Reports (CS-TR)

project was one of the earliest sustained investigation into the system engineering of digital libraries, and it pioneered multi-institutional collaborative research in this increasingly important area. The CS-TR project created a prototype digital library service that include a large collection of technical reports; an exchange format for bibliographic data.

CATRIONA II (https://catriona2.lib.strath.ac.uk/catriona/)

"The CATRIONA II project is an investigation of approaches to the managements and creation of institutional and departmental electronic resources in Scottish universities; of the existence of quality, locally-created, electronic resources on individual campuses and their value both within and beyond the local institution.

CORC—Corporative Online Resources Catalog (*http://www.library.oclc.org/cdm/ref/collection/p26770/*)

"CORC is a research project exploring the corporative creation and sharing of metadata by libraries and CORC is designed to help both libraries and OCLC to move more quickly in coping with the huge amount of material becoming available on the World Wide Web"

Nordic Metadata Projects (http://www.kansalliskirjasto.fi/extra/meta/)

The Nordic metadata project has started in Jan, 1999. The goal of the project is to design a shared metadata creation and utilization environment for digital documents. It emphasizes the importance of the participation of libraries in the process of cataloging.

Digital Library Projects of University of Illinois (*https://www.library.illinois.edu/digproj/digprojt.html*)

The UIUC Library and its departmental libraries carry out digital library activities, including the digitization of library collections and archive, research in information retrieval technologies for digital collections, and DL research projects.

Digital Library Project of University of California (*https://www.lib.berkeley.edu/node*)

"The project's goal is to develop the technologies for intelligent access to massive, distributed collection comprising multiple terabyte databases of photographs, satellite images, videos, maps.

Digital Library Project of University of Michigan (*http://www.lib.umich.edu/digital-librari-productional-service-dlps*)

"The content will emphasize diverse collection, focused on earth and space sciences, which can satisfy the needs of many different types of users. A related project, the Journal Storage Project (JSTOR), will digitize and make available all issues from the first publication through 1990 .

DIGITAL LIBRARY INITIATIVES IN UK

The Oxford Digital Library (ODL)

The Oxford Digital Library (ODL) offers Central access to Digital Collection of Oxford library. The Oxford Digital Library has a major role in Co-ordinating and stimulating digitization activities in the university. The Oxford Digital Library started operations in July 2001. The ODL is involved in following projects which are funded by the JISC.

- Complex archive Ingest for Repository object (CAIRO)
- Personal archives Accessible in Digital Media (Paradigm)
- Mest Awareness training Project
- The Early English Book Online project-the ODL is a partner in this project to encode 25,000 early printed books in XML.

- The Carte Calendar project- the ODL developed the guidelines and was responsible for delivering the encoded full-text for this conversion of a 19th century handwritten calendar to electronic form.
- Upcoming projects include the ECCO (Eighteen Century Collection Online) project

The PFI Project

The Digital Library Development Project aims to provide the Library with the capabilities to acquire, store, preserve and access collection material in digital form. It is expected that these developments will be achieved through partnering with the private sector using the Private Finance Initiative (PFI)

The Digital Data Store Development (3D)

The 3D Project was begun in1995 in an attempt to define the business and technical requirements for the library in developing its use of digital data. A substantial amount of work was carried out by contributors form across the Library in the second half of 1995 on defining business requirements.

Kentucky Digital Library

At the University of Kentucky, the Kentucky Digital Library project was initiated in 1997 and recently the Kentucky Digital Library was Chosen as one of six digital libraries to form the hub of pilot project.

Joint NSF/JISC International Digital Library Projects

In late 1998, the National Science Foundation in the United State and the UK Joint Information Systems Committee issued matching call for proposal for multi-country, multi-team projects that would involve at least one research team in the US and at least one in another country. Some of the projects funded so far are;

- Cross-Domain Resource Discovery

- HARMONY
- Online Music Recognition and Searching (OMRAS)
- Emulation option for digit preservation
- The I Mesh toolkit

DIGITAL LIBRARY INITIATIVE IN INDIA (DLI)

The concept of Digital Libraries (DL) and digitization has started in the western countries in the last couple of decades. The Digital Library of India (DLI) is one of the large scale digital library initiative in South Asia. Four mega scanning centres and 21 scanning centres are spread across the country to feed the digital contents into the digital library systems. Dr. A.P.J. Abdul Kalam, the former President of India, launched the portal of Digital Library of India on 8 September, 2003.

Digital Library of India project is a part of the Universal Digital Library (UDL) or Million Book Project, coordinated by the Carnegie Mellon University in United States of America. The National Science Foundation (USA) is providing funding for scanners and software research and development through Carnegie Mellon University. Varatharajan and Chandrashekhara (2007) discusses how Indian Institute of Science (IISc), Carnegie Mellon University (CMU), the International Institute of Information Technology, Hyderabad (IIITH), and other academic, religious, and government organizations in India have become partners in the Digital Library of India (DLI). The DLI seeks to preserve Indian heritage contained in books, manuscripts, art, and music. Each centre brings its own unique collection. A pilot project to scan some 10,000 books was initiated at CMU and then followed up at IISc, IIIT-H, IIIT-A and other organizations. The vision is to preserve all the knowledge of the human race in digital form and make that content searchable, independent of language and location, and to ensure that the cultural heritage of countries like India is not lost during the transition from paper to bits and bytes, as they were lost during a former transition of cultural content from palm leaves to paper. So far, more than 289,000 books have been scanned, of which nearly 170,000 are in Indian languages. More than 84,000 books (25 million pages) are available on the DLI web site at IISc, and more than 149,000 books (43 million pages) are available on the DLI web site at IIIT. The link to other partner sites is also provided through a commonly accessible website.

In their paper Bansode & Pujar (2008) described various digital library projects in India. Digital Library Projects can be categorized as "Government Institutions", "Academic Institutions", "Research Institutions" and "Religious Institutions", which are discussed in the below paragraphs.

GOVERNMENTS INSTITUTIONS

ERNET India (*http://www.ernet.in/about/abouternet.html*)

ERNET India is the National Research and Education Network dedicated to support the needs of the research and education community within the country. It was established in 1998 as an (DeitY), Government of India.

Indira Gandhi National centre for the Arts (IGNCA) (*http://ignca.nic.in/about.htm#AIMS*)

The IGNCA was launched on 19th November, 1985 to serve as a major resource centre for the arts, especially written, oral and visual source materials and to undertake research and publication programmes of reference works, glossaries, dictionaries and encyclopaedia.

State Central Library & Government press Mumbai (*www.digit.in/general/mumbai_is_now*)

Government of Maharashtra has opened the State Central Library & Government press Mumbai located in the Andheri. The library houses digital content in CD/

DVD/ROMs as well as various references and academic books in Hindi, Marathi and English.

State Central Library Hyderabad (*en.m.wikipedia.org/wiki/wiki_state_central_library_hyderabad*)

The state central library is a public library Began in 1981 in Hyderabad, Telangana. by "Nawab Imad ul Mulk" formerly known as "Asifiya Library" and was granted heritage status in 1998 by INTACH Hyderabad. It houses over 500,000 books and magazines in English, Hindi, Telugu, Tamil, Kannada, Marathi, Sanskrut, Urdu, Arabicand Persian. It has nearly 17,000 manuscripts.

ACADEMIC INSTITUTIONS

IIIT Allahabad (*www. iiita.ac.in*)

Indian Institute of Information Technology, Allahabad (IIITA) has been established in 1999 as a centre of excellence in IT and allied areas. The institute houses Regional Mega Scanning Centre for the Uttar Pradesh state. This mega scanning centre also coordinates digitization activities in different scanning centres across this region

IIAP-Bangalore (*www.prints.iiap.in*)

This digital repository of Indian Institute of Astrophysics (IIAP), Bangalore is developed to capture, organize disseminate and preserve the research publications of IIAP. It also includes the in-house technical reports and annual reports in addition to various other grey literatures created within the institute. The collection of IIAP includes archival records in various formats such as manuscripts, photographs, maps, films, awards, hand-drawn sketches, pictures and instruments.

Indian Institute of Technologies

Digital Library Initiative began in 1998 with faster

internet connection. IIT's receive grants from government bodies such as AICTE and Ministry of Human Resources Development (MHRD) to develop digital libraries. Following IIT institute in India are playing vital role in digitization work viz.

- Indian Institute of Technology, New Delhi, (1998):
- Indian Institute of Technology, Kharagpur (1994)
- Indian Institute of Technology, Bombay (1965)
- National Institute of Technology, Calicut /Nalanda Digital Library (1999)
- National Institute of Technology, Rourkela

Indian Institute of Science, Bangalore (*www.iisc.ernet.in*)

The IISc created institutional repositories using e-Prints an OSS. The archive is maintained by the National Center for Science Information (NCSI) and it supports self-archiving in various file formats, over 5,000 articles are available for access.

National Institute of Oceanography (*www.nio.org*)

The digital repository of the National Institute of Oceanography collects and preserves institutional publications such as journal articles, conference proceedings, technical reports, theses, dissertations, etc.

Indira Gandhi Memorial Library (*Igmlnet.uohyd.ernet.in:8000/*)

The Indira Gandhi Memorial Library, University of Hyderabad has digitized around 250,000 pages, primarily theses ~~are~~ and dissertations, as well as 300 books in English and Indian languages.

RESEARCH INSTITUTIONS

Raman Research Institute (*www.dspace.rri.res.in*)

The Raman Research Institute Digital Repository allows the institute community to deposit preprints, post-prints, and other publications.

CDAC-Kolkata

The Centre for Development of Advanced Computing (CDAC) Kolkata hosts Regional Mega Scanning Centre for the eastern zone of India. This Regional Mega Scanning Centre has a centralized digitization facility where some source libraries will send their books for digitization.

Academy of Sanskrit Research (ASR) (*www.caravanmagzine.in/vantage/GRJ_academy_sanskrit_research*)

ASR is situated at the Melkote being the place where Ramanujacharya residual for 12 years & propagated the visistadvaita philosophy, naturally most of the research work in the academy center revolves around Vedanta & its relevance.

RELIGIOUS INSTITUTIONS

Sharda Peetham, Sringeri (*http://www.sringeri.net/activities/education/scholarship-library-research-and-propogation*)

The Mutt has library at Sringeri consisting of ancient as well as the present work. The mutt carries on the activity of propagation of Shankara philosophy, ancient literature, yoga, ayurveda, sanskrit, spiritual and moral education.

TTD-Tirupati (*www.tirumala.org/digitallibrary.aspx*)

S.V. Digital Library of T.T.D. in association with Universal Digital Library and Carnegie Mellon University, Pittsburgh, U.S.A established TTD - Tirupati with a view to digitize the rare and ancients books, scriptures, palm leaves. At present nearly 60,000 books are scanned and all the books are kept in web for accessing.

PILOT PROJECTS INITIATED IN INDIA

Traditional Knowledge Digital Library (TKDL)

Traditional Knowledge Digital Library (TKDL) is collaborative project between the National Institute of Science Communication and Information Resources (NISCAIR) and the Council of Scientific and Industrial Research (CSIR), Ministry of Science and technology. The TKDL project involves documentation of knowledge available in public domain on traditional knowledge from the existing literature related to Ayurveda, Unani and Siddha, in digitized format in five international languages viz., English, German, French, Japanese, and Spanish.

Vidyanidhi

Vidyanidhi began as a pilot project in the year 2000 with the support from the National Information System for Science and Technology (NISSAT) and the Government of India's Department of Scientific and Industrial Research (DSIR). Vidyanidhi project evolved as a national repository and a consortium for e-theses through participation from universities, academic institutions and other stake holders.

Electronic Theses and Dissertation Project of INFLIBNET Centre (*www.dspace.inflibnet.ac.in*)

INLIBNET hosts a bibliographic database consists of over 200,000 dissertations from about two hundred Indian universities. The Repository uses DSpace, which complies with the Open Archives Initiative (OAI) framework allowing publications to be easily indexed and searched by web search engines and other indexing services.

Kalasampada (*www.ignca.gov.in/dgt.000/.html*)

IGNCA has taken up the Kalasampada Digital Library – Resoruce for Indian Cultural Heritage (DL-RICH) project, which is sponsored by the Ministry of

Communication and Information Technology (MCIT). Kalasampada will facilitate access for students, research scholars, artists, and scientific community. The materials include several hundred thousand manuscripts, more than one hundred thousand slides, thousands of rare books, photographs, audio and video.

V.V. Giri National Labour Institute (*www.indialabourarchives.org*)

The Archives of Indian Labour is the joint initiative of V.V. Giri National Labour Institute and the Association of Indian Labour Historians (AILH). The archive preserves documents, builds collections, and initiates research in labour history.

Indian Parliament Library (*www.parliamentofindia.nic.in*)

This library serves members of Parliament and officers and staff of Loksabha Secretariat. Large databases were initially developed by the computer centre. The data are stored and available now in PARLIS (Parliament Library Information System).

Khudabaksh Oriental Public Library (*www.kblibrary.org*)

This library has rich collection of manuscripts in Persian, Arabic, Urdu and other languages.

The descriptive catalogue is available in a 30-volume set which appeared in 1923 and was reprinted in the 1970s.

DIGITAL LIBRARY INITIATIVE AT NATIONAL LIBRARY OF INDIA

This is a permanent repository of all material produced in India and written by Indians. The Library started a digitization project of publication in English and other European languages. It also has a rich collection of Sanskrit, Persian, Arabic and Tamil manuscripts.

DIGITAL LIBRARY ISSUES

There are number of problems the Digital Library development teams face in India. Some of them are as follows.

Technological Issues : Library need to upgrade IT infrastructure, high speed Internet connectivity etc.

Creating Digital Collection : Acquiring original digital work while digitizing existing material is one of the main challenges faced by the libraries.

Planning /integration of digital resources : For planning of electronic resources it needs framed content integrated model.

Publisher's Policy : For successfully installed and configured library one has to obtain publisher's permission. Publisher put the standard digital format such as HTML, RTF, PPT, PDF or Word so the text extraction almost impossible without the permission of publisher.

Strategies and Policy : Most of the libraries do not have their own policy, but they need to have their own strategies and policies to meet the issues posed by the technology.

Technical Skill : The human resources of libraries need professional enrichment inputs from time-to-time on the latest technologies.

Management support : For establishment of world class information systems libraries need financial support from the respective management.

Copyright / IPR Issues : Issues of copyright, and fair use concerns are posing array of problems to the libraries and librarians are struggling to manage these issues.

CONCLUSION

The developed countries such as UK and USA have

proper support from their government as well as private funding to give them adequate financial support. The developing country like India though facing fund crunch for digitization work but have made gradual progress in this direction with financial support from; CSIR, NISCAIR, various Ministries of Govt. of India shows a greater effort towards the initiation of digital library projects, as a result many projects are completed and many more projects are in progress.

The Digital Library projects in India, UK, and USA has a bright future and great achievement to give their user's better services through Digitization of library materials, providing services on the desktop of each and every user. It is observed that not only Government resources are fully digitized but academic as well as Religious Institutions are well digitized it means that the effort has come from all the area of society. And also it is observed that Digital Library of India initiative provides many opportunities to all segments of learners and readers, including persons located in remote places but having access to ICT facilities at their neighborhoods.

REFERENCES

Babbar, P &Jain, P.K.(2006).Digital libraries initiatives in India. The *International Information and Library Review, 38*, 161-169.

Bansode, S. & Pujar, S. M. (2008). Scholarly digital library initiatives: World Vs India. *DESIDOC Journal of Library and Information Technology, 28*(6), 21-26.

CATRIONA II: Approaches to University Management of Electronic Resources. (n.d.)

CATRIONA project [data file] Retrieved from *http://www.ukoln.ac.uk/services/elib/projects/catriona/*

Das, Anup Kumar. (2008). An evaluation study of some selected libraries in India undergoing the process of digitization (Unpublished thesis). Jadavpur University, Kolkata.

Hickey, B.T. (2001). CORE-Cooperative online resource catalog. *Journal of Library Administration, 34*(3-4), 112-116.

IMS Learning Resource Meta-data Information Model (Version 1.1). (n.d.). IMS project [data file]. Retrieved from *http://www.imsproject.org/metadata/mdinfov1p1.pdf*

Info librarian (1996). The public-access computer system review. A*n electronic journal of the University of Houston Libraries,* 7(2). Retrieved from *http://info.lib.uh.edu/pr/v7/n2/ande7n2.html*

Latin Americanist Research Resources Project. (n.d.). Center for Research Libraries Global Resources Network [data file]. Retrieved from *https://Lanic.utexas.edu/project/*

Mahendrakar, S. (2011). State of digital library initiative in engineering and technology collage libraries. *VSRD Technical and non Technical Journal, 2* (9), 451-461.

Munchen, K. G.(1998). Functional requirements for bibliographic records, IFLA Study Group on the Function Requirement for Bibliographic Records [IFLA Module] Retrieved from http://www.ifla.org/VII/s13/frbr/frbr.htm

Philip, Hunter. (1997). The British libraries private finance initiative. *Ariadne* Issue Retrieved from *https://www.ariadne.ac.uk/issue7/british-library/*

Varatharajan, N. & Jain, P. K. (2007). Digital library initiatives at higher education and research institutions in India *.Library Philosophy and Practice, 6,* 1-7.

Website used :

http://www.dli.gov.in/

http://www.open.gov./citu

http://www.iitd.ac.in/

http://iitkgp.ernet.in/

http://library.iitb.ac.in

www.dli.ernet.in/

http://www.dlib.org/projects.html#national

http://www.dlib.washington.edu/digital/

www.odl.ox.ac.uk

http://www.itcompany.com/inforetriever/projrct.htm

http://dlib.org/dlib.org/dlib/june99/06wiseman.html

http://www.dli2.nsf.gov>

http://www.library.oclc.org/cdm/ref/collection/p297701coll27/id/133

http://www.kansalliskrirjasto.fi/extra/muut/meta/

http://www.lib.berkeley.edu/node

www.library.illinois.edu>library>Digital Projects

http://www.lib.umich.edu/digital-library-production-service-dlps

http://www.emeraldinsight.com/doi.abs/10.1108/07378839

http://dublincore.org/documents/dces/

http://www.informedia.cs.cmu.edu/timeline/index.html

http://infopeople.org

http://www.bodley.ox.ac.uk/ilej/

http://www.muse-project.eu/

http://digilib.stanford.edu:8091/

http://lanic.utexas.edu/project

http://www.iisc.ernet.in

Index